Guide to California Government

Fourteenth Edition
1992

League of Women Voters of California
Education Fund
926 J Street, #1000
Sacramento, CA 95814

Acknowledgements

The fourteenth edition of *Guide to California Government* is the result of the diligent efforts of many people. First, our profound thanks to the many persons in California government who contributed their time and expertise in ensuring that this book is not only comprehensive, but thoroughly accurate.

MMC Communications served as overall project coordinator for research, editing, and production. Adam Gottlieb deserves special recognition for the thoroughness of his research and his unfailing ability to track down information. Janet Grossman's keen eye was also essential in final copy editing.

Creative Copy provided the cover artwork, book layout, and developed lively presentations of the various charts and graphs.

Last, but far from least, Virginia Birdsall, LWVCEF Executive Vice President, served as project director, providing everyone involved with the clear direction and meticulous oversight so important in an effort as significant as this book.

ISBN 0-9632465-0-X

Preface

If citizens are to participate effectively in democratic government, it is essential that they know something about the structure of government — how government is organized, what services it provides, what costs it entails, and how citizens can affect governmental decisions.

For more than 72 years the League of Women Voters of California has worked to encourage a close relationship between citizens and their government. Towards this end, for more than 52 years it has published a government handbook for student and citizen use.

This *Guide to California Government* is the fourteenth edition of that handbook. Its purpose is to provide comprehensive yet concise information on the structure and functions of government in California.

Efforts have been made to bring the reader as up-to-date as possible. The information presented here is that which was current and available as of February 1992.

Robyn Prud'homme-Bauer
President
League of Women Voters of California
Education Fund

TABLE OF CONTENTS

FIGURES

LAYING
THE
FOUNDATIONS

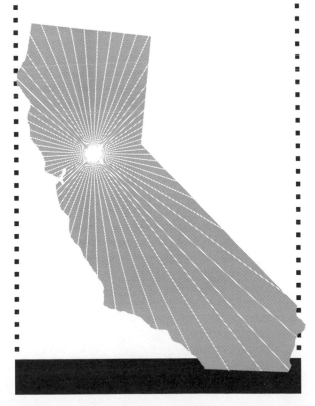

GOVERNMENT BY CONSTITUTION

BEFORE STATEHOOD

In 1769, when Spain first began permanent settlements in the isolated land of present-day California, Upper (Alta) and Lower (Baja) California were both under control of one governor who ruled from Loreto in Lower California. As soldiers and Franciscan missionaries moved north, local government evolved with *commandantes* given control over the military establishments (*presidios*), and padres given authority over the missions and towns (*pueblos*) that grew up around them.

In 1777, while English colonists on the eastern seaboard rebelled against their sovereign, on the west coast Spain moved the capital of its colony from Loreto to Monterey in recognition of Alta California's growing importance. In that same year, the first civil pueblo was established in San Jose and was governed by a mayor (*alcalde*) and town council. Alta California continued to grow with *presidios* at San Diego, Santa Barbara, Monterey, and San Francisco. The missions stretched along the coast from San Diego to Sonoma, and another civil *pueblo* was established in Los Angeles.

With the success of the Mexican revolution in 1821, California came under Mexican rather than Spanish rule. This change in authority brought little change in government. It was difficult to develop stable government with a population of widely scattered soldiers, priests, and independent colonists. The military *commandantes* constantly challenged the authority of the governors sent out from Mexico. Local civil disputes were settled by the *alcalde*, who was chosen locally but was replaced almost at whim. Although missions were founded with the intent of "civilizing" the Indians, granting them Mexican citizenship, and turning the mission towns into civil communities, this plan for secularization never proceeded on schedule. Disputes over land ownership added to the tumult and conflict that marked this period of California history. As resentment against neglect and indifference by the Mexican government grew, Californians came to think of themselves as *"Californios"* rather than Mexicans, and Mexican governors were chased out of the province with increasing frequency.

Mexican control of California lasted for fewer than 20 years. In 1846 the dispute over Texas led the United States to declare war on Mexico. When the war ended, the Treaty of Guadalupe Hidalgo officially ceded Upper California to the United States, provided for U.S. Citizenship for Mexican Californians, and upheld the validity of Mexican land grants.

CONSTITUTION OF 1849

Because California's future had become a part of the bitter dispute over slavery, three successive sessions of Congress—the last in 1849—adjourned without arriving at a decision on statehood. Meanwhile, government was chaotic; in many areas there was not even the meager stability of the local *alcalde* system. With the discovery of gold and resultant immigration, the demand grew for a firmly established government.

In 1849, the military governor called for a constitutional convention to meet in Monterey in September. Of the 48 delegates, only 13 were over 40 years of age; nine were under 30. Three fourths of the men were immigrants from other states; eight of them had lived in California less than a year. In contrast, seven of the eight Spanish-surname delegates had lived in California all their lives. All were men in a hurry to get their business done.

The constitution they drafted showed substantial borrowings from the U.S. Constitution and those of other states. The Declaration of Rights stated that all men are free and independent, and that political power is inherent in the people. It incorporated the protections of the federal Bill of Rights and forbade slavery. Suffrage was granted to male citizens. The legislature was authorized to extend the vote to Indians, and did so in its first session. The executive department of the government was headed by the same statewide officials as today, with the addition of a surveyor general to help resolve continuing conflicts over land ownership. Four levels of courts were established. The legislature was divided into two houses; sessions were to be held annually. Few directions or prohibitions were imposed on the legislature, although considerable restraints were placed on corporations and banks. The legislature was to provide for county and city government. It could incur debt beyond $300,000 only with voter approval. Taxation was to be uniform; assessors were to be locally elected. A wife's separate property was protected, and homesteads were protected from forced sale. All laws were to be published in both English and Spanish.

The delegates convened in September and adjourned in October. The constitution was overwhelmingly ratified in November, with the first elected governor taking office in December 1849. The legislature met, set up a tax system, established counties, provided for a court system, and borrowed $200,000 to get under way. The government was operating, but California was not yet a state. It was not until September 9, 1850, that Congress admitted California to the union as the thirty-first state.

CONSTITUTION OF 1879

In the 30 years between 1849 and 1879, inadequacies in the constitution became increasingly apparent. Controls over state spending were almost nonexistent. The powerful railroad bloc dominated government in general and the legislature in particular. California's population had exploded; for every 100 persons who had been in the state in 1849, there were 1,700 by 1879. With an economic depression and a prolonged drought, many were unemployed. Unrest was general. Farmers were in revolt against railroads and other large businesses. A Workingman's Party had formed to protest imported Chinese labor, and the farmers supported the new party's effort to reform the constitution.

In 1877, voters approved a proposal for a new constitutional convention. The delegates to the 1878 convention worked for five months and drew up the longest of all state constitutions. To correct omissions in the first constitution, they introduced severe restrictions on all branches of state government, particularly on the legislature. The judiciary was completely reorganized. Restrictions were placed on the governor's pardoning power. New provisions made home rule charters available to cities. All property, tangible or intangible, became subject to taxation. Operations of public utilities, railroads, and other corporations were regulated. The rights of Chinese were abridged to a degree which the U.S. Supreme Court later found unconstitutional. Opinion was sharply divided on the new constitution, but it was adopted in 1879 by a solid margin.

For all its detail, the new constitution produced few of the desired reforms. These came later, as the Progressive Movement (1910-1916) gave the people a new means of reform through the initiative, referendum, recall, and direct primary.

CHANGING THE CONSTITUTION

The California Constitution may be changed in three ways: amendment, constitutional convention, or revision proposed by the legislature.

By far the most common method of change is by amendment. The legislature may place an amendment on the ballot by a two-thirds vote of the members of each house, or citizens may do so by the initiative process. Since 1884, about 445 amendments had been adopted out of more than 685 proposed by the legislature. In the same period, 35 initiative constitutional amendments had been adopted out of a total of 115 proposed.

The legislature, by a two-thirds vote of each house, may also propose a convention to change the constitution. If the voters approve, the legislature must provide for the convention within six months. California has not held a constitutional convention since 1878. Three proposals have been turned down at the polls; in 1934 a fourth passed, but the legislature took no action to call the convention or to give it financial support.

The California Constitution of 1879 has been amended literally hundreds of times in an effort to update matters which in most states are left to ordinary legislation and are therefore more easily changed. On two occasions large quantities of obsolete provisions were methodically deleted; nevertheless the document grew from 16,000 to 75,000 words.

Finally, a 1962 amendment provided a new method for securing more than piecemeal change. It permitted the legislature, by a vote of two-thirds of each house, to submit to the people either a partial or total revision of the constitution. A constitution revision commission, composed primarily of citizen representatives, worked for seven years to study and modernize the entire document. Ambiguities and dated language were removed and more flexibility introduced by deleting details and expressly authorizing new options. The number of words was cut in half. Three-fourths of the proposed revisions were accepted by the legislature and the voters over a period of ten years.

With an average of seven newly proposed constitutional amendments on every state ballot, the California Constitution is a document which continues to grow in scope and length.

EXERCISING CITIZEN RIGHTS

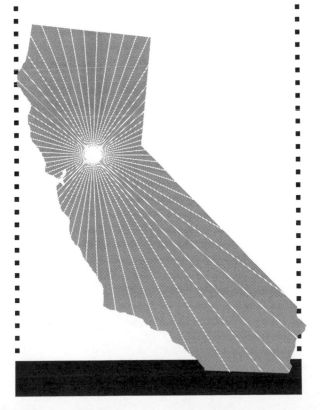

2

VOTERS
AND
ELECTIONS

The constitution of both the United States and California specifically protect the right to vote. Representative democracy ultimately rests on the fact that citizens elect those who make and administer the laws.

WHO MAY VOTE

Anyone may vote who is

- a U.S. Citizen
- at least 18 years of age
- a resident of California
- a resident of the precinct for at least 29 days before the election
- registered to vote

Figure 2.1

VOTER QUALIFICATIONS AND REGISTRATION

The general qualifications for voters are listed in **Figure 2.1**. There are a few exceptions to these requirements. Persons declared mentally incompetent cannot vote; convicted felons cannot vote while incarcerated or on parole. If a voter has recently moved and has not lived in the new precinct for 29 days, he or she may still vote by absentee ballot or by returning to the old polling place. A new state resident need not meet the residence requirements in order to vote for President of the United States. The new resident may apply for a presidential ballot from the county clerk or registrar of voters up until seven days before the election.

HOW TO REGISTER
California election laws are designed to encourage registration and maintain it at the highest possible level. Voters may register by official

postcards which may be obtained from the county clerk or registrar of voters or at various locations such as post offices. Citizens may also call (800) 345-VOTE to request voter registration cards be sent to their households. A citizen may register at any time, but must be registered for 29 days before being permitted to vote. The prospective voter fills out an affidavit of registration, supplying name, address, citizenship, date of birth, and political party affiliation, if any. There is no charge for registration. The applicant mails the completed form to the county elections official who then sends a card back verifying the registration. Completed forms may also be left with the registrant for return to the elections office. If delivered by a third party, the registration form must be received by the elections official within three days of being completed.

A person who indicates a political party preference at the time of registration is entitled to vote in the primary election when that party's candidates are selected. A voter who "declines to state" a party affiliation when registering to vote will receive a primary ballot listing only ballot propositions and the names of candidates for nonpartisan offices. An unaffiliated voter, therefore, cannot vote in the primary to select party candidates for offices such as president, governor, senator, or state legislator. In the general election, however, all voters may cast ballots for candidates of any political party.

California has permanent voter registration. A voter must re-register only if changing his or her name, address, or party affiliation. Failure to vote does not disqualify a voter's registration.

ABSENTEE VOTING

Any voter may apply for an absentee ballot; no special reason is required. Applications may be made any time up to seven days before an election. Political parties or campaign committees may also distribute absentee ballot applications. Recent elections have seen an increase in the use of absentee ballots as a political campaign tool. Outcomes for several state Assembly, state Senate and congressional races would have been decided differently if not for extensive absentee balloting efforts. Ballots are mailed to those requesting them seven to 29 days before the election. They may be returned by mail or in person. A voted absentee ballot may also be turned in at any polling place in the county on election day. All absentee ballots must be received by the time the polls close.

If a voter is unable to get to the polls because of conditions arising when it is too late to apply for an absentee ballot by mail, he or she may still obtain one as late as election day from the office of the county elections official. If the voter is confined at home or in a hospital, someone with written authorization from the voter may obtain a ballot for him or her and return it before the polls close.

An absentee ballot remains a secret ballot and must be enclosed in a sealed envelope. Election officials are required to verify that the

FEDERAL AND STATE OFFICIALS ELECTED BY CALIFORNIA VOTERS

PARTISAN OFFICES

National Level	Elected by	Term	Election Year
President	Entire state	4 years	Years divisible by four
U.S. Senators	Entire state	6 years	Every six years counting from 1992
			Every six years counting from 1994
Members of Congress	Districts	2 years	Even-numbered years
State Level			
Governor[1]			
Lt. Governor[1]			
Secretary of State[1]	Entire state	4 years	Even-numbered years when there is no presidential election
Controller[1]			
Treasurer[1]			
Attorney General[1]			
Insurance Commissioner			
Members of Board of Equalization[1]	Districts	4 years	Same as governor
State Senators[1]	Districts	4 years	Same as governor for even-numbered districts
			Same as president for odd-numbered districts
Assembly members[2]	Districts	2 years	Even-numbered years.

NONPARTISAN OFFICES

State Level			
Superintendent of Public Instruction	Entire state	4 years	Same as governor
Supreme Court justices	Entire state	12 years	Same as governor
Court of Appeal justices	Entire state	12 years	Same as governor
Superior Court judges	Counties	6 years	Even-numbered years

[1] - Limited to two terms by Proposition 140.
[2] - Limited to three terms by Proposition 140.

Figure 2.2

signature on the absentee ballot is the voter's actual signature before the vote is counted.

ELECTIONS

Citizens go to the polls to choose many local officials. They may also directly elect some federal and state officials, as indicated in **Figure 2.2.**

ELECTION OFFICIALS

The secretary of state is the chief elections officer of California.

The county board of supervisors serves as a board of election commissioners for a county; the governing body of a city serves for the city. These two boards are responsible for the conduct of all elections in the county. In many counties the county clerk administers the election process; in more populous counties a registrar of voters heads a separate elections department.

Precincts are small voting districts created to make voting convenient and to make possible a quick counting of votes. The county elections official creates, alters, or consolidates precincts as necessary due to changes in population or district boundaries.

Precinct boards staff the polls on election day. Precinct board members are citizens who are selected by the county elections official and receive a small stipend for their work on election day. Any voter may apply for appointment as an elections officer.

Federal law requires bilingual assistance at polling places when more than five percent of the citizens of voting age in a political subdivision are of a single language minority group and do not understand English well enough to participate in the electoral process. In 1992, election materials in Spanish had to be provided in ten counties in California: Fresno, Imperial, Kern, Kings, Madera, Merced, Monterey, San Benito, Tulare, and Yuba. The English-only ballot initiative passed in 1984 was advisory only; it required the governor to urge U.S. officials to amend federal law to eliminate foreign language voting materials.

BALLOT MEASURES

In addition to names of candidates, California ballots usually include several ballot measures. The state constitution requires a vote of the people on any general obligation bond act or proposal to change the constitution. Such measures must receive a two-thirds vote in each house of the legislature before they are placed on the ballot. In addition to propositions initiated by the legislature, initiatives and referendums may appear on the ballot by direct action of the people.

A majority vote is required for passage of all state ballot measures. Unless the measure itself provides otherwise, a newly passed measure goes into effect the day after the election. In cities, counties, and school districts, a majority vote is required to pass local ballot measures and charter changes.

INFORMATION FOR VOTERS

Before an election, the secretary of state compiles a ballot pamphlet containing the complete text of all proposed constitutional amendments, bond measures, initiatives and referendums. The pamphlet includes a copy of any provisions then in force which would be amended by the proposals, the legislative analyst's summary of the proposals and their fiscal effects, arguments for and against each measure, and rebuttals.

Before printing and mailing, a draft of the state ballot pamphlet is available for public examination in Sacramento. Any voter may challenge in court the accuracy of this information and request corrections. The secretary of state then mails a ballot pamphlet to the household of each voter registered 60 days or more before an election. County clerks mail pamphlets to those who register between that date and the close of registration (29 days before an election).

When a ballot proposition originates in the legislature, the author of the bill generally writes the "pro" argument. A legislator who voted against the bill is asked to write the "con" argument. Sometimes other persons co-author the pro or con arguments with the legislators. When a measure passes unanimously, the secretary of state solicits opposing arguments from citizens. If there is no response to this request, no opposing argument appears in the pamphlet. In the case of initiatives and referendums, the citizens sponsoring the measure write the pro arguments. The secretary of state selects opposing arguments from among those submitted by various groups or individuals. Preference is given to bona fide citizens groups.

In each county, the clerk/registrar compiles ballot pamphlets and sample ballots and distributes them so that each voter receives voting information on local candidates and measures which are on the ballot in his or her particular precinct. Arguments for and against any local measure are solicited by the clerk/registrar. In county elections, preference must be given to arguments submitted by members of the board of supervisors. Next preference is given to arguments by groups formed specifically to support or oppose the measure, followed by arguments of citizen associations. Arguments of individual citizens are chosen last. Candidates' statements, printed at their expense, may be included in local pamphlets.

ELECTION DAY

Election day practices and procedures are designed to encourage voting, to protect against fraud, and to ensure that no vote is invalidated because of the voter's lack of knowledge of the process.

To accommodate as many voters as possible, the polls open early, at 7 A.M., and close at 8 P.M. Anyone who arrives at their designated polling place before closing time and is waiting in line may vote after 8 P.M. When a voting machine is used, an election official must offer to instruct the voter on its use. Booths may not be occupied by more than one person at a time, except for persons assisting voters with disabilities. A voter who spoils a ballot by making an error may return it and receive another. A voter may get two ballots in addition to the original, but no more than three. Spoiled ballots are cancelled by election officials and returned with the unused ballots; the election board must account for every ballot delivered to it.

A voter may be challenged as to identity, on the basis of having already voted, or on the basis of residence or other qualifications. Only a precinct official may challenge a voter, although any voter may have a challenge presented through a precinct board member. The challenged voter is allowed to vote only after satisfactorily answering certain questions under oath. Any doubt in the interpretation of the law is resolved in the favor of the challenged voter.

The precinct board must post outside the polling place an index of persons registered to vote in that precinct, listing voter's name, address, and, party affiliation. Throughout the day precinct officials cross off the names of those who have voted. Often supporters or opponents of candidates or ballot measures check the index and remind those who have not voted to come to the polls.

Other laws ensure the voter's independence in casting a vote. Bribery, intimidation and defrauding of voters, voting when not entitled to, tampering with voting equipment, and altering election returns are all illegal activities. The law forbids anyone within 100 feet of a polling place from electioneering or speaking to a voter about his or her vote.

While secrecy is protected in marking ballots, openness is emphasized in counting them. Procedures differ, depending on whether electronic or mechanical devices are used, and whether votes are counted at a central place, but the steps in each method are prescribed by law, and every step must be taken in public view of official observers. Any voter may be present, but may not interfere. Absentee ballots are

ELECTION CALENDAR		
Type of Election	Month	Year
Primary	June	Even-numbered years
General	November	Even-numbered years
Municipal		
General law cities	April	Even-numbered years
Charter cities*	March	Odd-numbered years
	April	Even-numbered years
School Districts *	November	Odd-numbered years
Special Districts	November	Odd-numbered years
* with some exceptions		

Figure 2.3

counted on election day at the office of the county elections official. Any election may be contested and a recount requested.

PRIMARY ELECTIONS

Primaries are held on the first Tuesday after the first Monday in June in even-numbered years, as indicated in **Figure 2.3**.

The direct party primary is basically an election to nominate. A voter whose registration indicates a party affiliation may vote on that party's ballot to select its candidates for the general election. Only registered Democrats may vote in the Democratic primary. Similarly, only registered Republicans may vote in the Republican primary. Registered third party voters also elect their candidates at this time.

When a presidential primary is consolidated with the regular primary, voters may also choose delegates to their party's national convention. Under the Republican, "winner-take-all" system, all delegates go to the primary winner. Democrats do not permit winner-take-all primaries.

Delegates are not selected as individuals, but as a slate pledged to support a particular presidential candidate. Slates may also be unpledged, or unaffiliated with any of the listed candidates.

While a political candidate for a nonpartisan office may be a member of a political party, he or she cannot list a party affiliation on the ballot. Many nonpartisan officers are selected at the primary election, including the state superintendent of public instruction and county officials. A candidate for a nonpartisan office who receives a majority of all ballots cast for that office is elected outright. If no one receives more than 50 percent, the two candidates with the greatest number of votes run against each other in the general election.

A voter whose registration indicates no party preference receives a primary ballot which contains only ballot measures and the names of candidates for nonpartisan office.

GENERAL ELECTIONS

General elections are held on the first Tuesday after the first Monday in November, as indicated in **Figure 2.3**.

Ballots in the general election do not differ by party. Every voter selects from among all candidates, those nominated by the political parties in the June primary and those filed as independents. Votes also are cast on ballot measures and various nonpartisan offices, including most judgeships and posts where a run-off was required after the primary.

SPECIAL ELECTIONS

Special elections are called when a vacancy must be filled, a recall voted on, or a public decision be made earlier than the time of the next regular election. For economy and voter convenience, special elections are often consolidated with regularly scheduled elections.

The governor may call a special election to fill a vacancy in state and congressional offices or to determine a statewide issue (except for bond measures). The governing body of a county, city, or school district may call a special election to fill a vacancy or vote on a bond act, charter question, or other ballot measure.

An election to fill a vacancy must be scheduled not less than 112 days nor more than 119 days following the proclamation calling for the special election. A primary election is held on the eighth Tuesday before the special election. A candidate receiving more than 50 percent of the votes cast is elected. If no candidate has a majority, the candidates who receive the highest vote in each party compete at the special election.

RECALL ELECTIONS

The state constitution guarantees the power of the voters to remove any state or local elective official from office. There are two major steps in any recall procedure. The first is circulation of a petition for signatures of persons qualified to vote for the office in question, asking for a recall election. The second is an election to decide two separate questions, whether the incumbent shall be recalled and, if so, who shall succeed the officeholder.

A recall petition must contain a statement of the reasons for which the recall is sought. There is no requirement for specific charges; any reason is acceptable. In contrast to the impeachment process, an official subject to recall need not have violated the law.

A petition to recall an officer who has been elected statewide must be signed by voters equal to 12 percent of the most recent total vote for that office with signatures from each of five counties equal to one percent of the last vote for that office in that county. A petition to recall a state legislator, judge, or member of the Board of Equalization must have signatures equal to 20 percent of the last vote for the office. Recall proponents have 160 days in which to file the signed petitions. The governor must call an election to be held between 60 and 80 days after the secretary of state certifies that enough signatures have been collected.

A candidate who wishes to replace a recalled official must file a declaration of candidacy and nomination documents (as if filing for a regular election) 68 days or more before the election. The person subject to the recall may not be a candidate in the replacement election.

If a majority votes in favor of recall, the officer is removed and the candidate receiving more votes than any other candidate becomes the successor. A vote on the recall question is counted whether or not a vote is cast for one of the replacement candidates. However, a vote for a replacement candidate will be counted only if the voter answers the question on recall. A vacancy created by the recall of a judge is filled by the governor or, in the case of a justice court, by the board of supervisors.

In California the recall process has been used mostly at the local level. Local governments may adopt their own recall procedures, but state law sets certain requirements. Local governments are prohibited from requiring recall petition signatures totaling more than 25 percent of the vote cast in the last election for the office involved. A minimum of 20 percent is set for recalls in general law counties and 12 percent for general law cities.

3

CANDIDATES AND POLITICAL PARTIES

In California, as elsewhere, representative democracy depends upon concerned citizens being willing to serve in public office and spend the energy, time, and money required to campaign for office. Political parties provide the machinery through which citizens choose who will govern their state and nation. Voters directly select all legislative officers. By directly electing executive officers, voters determine who will appoint other policy-making officials.

California law sets qualifications and regulates expenditures of candidates; it also regulates the structure and functions of political parties.

THE CANDIDATE

Any candidate must meet requirements of age, residence, and citizenship. Eighteen is the minimum age for candidates for state and local office. Candidates for governor and lieutenant governor must have been U.S. citizens for five years and residents of California for five years immediately preceding the election. There are no constitutional requirements for any other state executive officers. A candidate for the state Senate or Assembly must have been a U.S. citizen for three years, a resident of the state for three years, and a resident of the legislative district when nomination documents are issued.

Several steps are involved in getting one's name on the ballot. Candidates for all offices must file declarations of candidacy and nomination documents signed by a specified number of voters. A candidate for any partisan state executive position must file a petition signed by at least 65 registered voters belonging to his or her political party. A candidate for state Senate or Assembly needs at least 40 signatures. Candidates for local nonpartisan offices need even fewer signatures. For a county board of supervisors, for example, "not less than 20 nor more than 30 signatures" are needed.

A candidate who is not affiliated with a political party and wishes to run for a partisan office may not participate in the primary election. He or she, however, may qualify for the general election ballot, but the number of required signatures is much higher–134,781 or one percent of statewide voter registration to run for statewide office. A write-in candidate must file both a declaration of candidacy and nomination documents two weeks before a state election (or eight days before a local election) in order for his or her votes to be counted.

All candidates are also required to pay filing fees which vary depending on the office. However, candidates may elect to defray all or part of the filing fees by gathering signatures on petitions for that purpose.

CAMPAIGN FINANCING

Campaign financing is a major concern of any candidate for public office. There is no legal limit on the amount that can be spent. The cost of campaigning for elective office in California has drastically increased; in recent years more than $20 million has been spent by a single candidate for a statewide office. During the 1990 gubernatorial election, an aggregate total of $43 million was spent by candidates Pete Wilson and Dianne Feinstein. By comparison, George Deukmejian and Tom Bradley spent a combined $22.5 million in the 1986 gubernatorial election. The median cost of a 1990 state Senate race was $713,974 and the median cost of a state Assembly race was $347,324.

The California personal income tax law encourages political donations by allowing a deduction of $100 per person for contributions to candidates in a primary or general election. It also allows up to $25 of an income tax refund to be directed to a political party.

The Political Reform Act of 1974 requires extensive reports on campaign financing of state and local candidates in order that the public may know the source of a candidate's funds. The act also regulates lobbyists and defines conflict of interest. Any committee that receives or spends $1,000 in a year to support or oppose a candidate or ballot measure must file a statement of organization with the secretary of state. Since 1989, candidates for elective office must also file forms stating their intention to receive or to solicit campaign funds. All candidates must have a separate bank account for any campaign. Each committee's treasurer is accountable for its contributions and expenditures. A candidate must file a statement if *any* money, including the candidate's personal funds, is received or spent. A candidate may not use campaign funds for personal use.

A *report of contributions and expenditures* must be filed by a candidate at least three times during an election period. Campaign committees must file campaign disclosure statements twice during the election and once afterward. This applies to campaigns for candidates, as well as those for and against ballot measures. In all campaign reports each contribution of $100 or more in money, goods, or services must be listed with the name, address, occupation, and employer of the contributor. All expenditures of $100 or more must be itemized. Contributions or expenditures of $100 or more may not be made in cash. Anonymous contributions over $100 are prohibited.

The Franchise Tax Board performs mandatory audits of all reports of all statewide and Board of Equalization candidates and candidates for the Supreme Court and Courts of Appeal who have raised or spent at least $25,000. Political action committees, or PACs, are also subject to audits.

Conflict of interest provisions are designed to ensure that public officials do not participate in governmental decisions in which they have a financial interest. An official is considered to have a financial interest if he or she has a direct or indirect interest worth more than $1,000 in a business or real property, is an officer or employee in a business, or receives income of more than $250 from an affected party within 12 months before a decision is made.

Conflict of interest provisions apply not only to all elected officials at all levels of government, but also to many high level appointees, such as senior university officials, city managers, district attorneys, judges, and, members of some boards and commissions. In addition, staff members of elected officials may also be subject to conflict of interest provisions.

A candidate must file a financial disclosure statement with the original declaration of candidacy. Officeholders must file a statement within 30 days after assuming office and annually thereafter. These statements describe the nature of investments, value of real property, and income including gifts.

With the passage of Proposition 112 by the voters in June 1990, *elected* state officers are no longer able to accept gifts with a value of more than $250 from a single source in a calender year nor accept any honorarium. Elected local officers may not accept gifts or honoraria whose aggregate total is more than $1,000 from a single source in a calender year. Honorarium is defined as, "any payment made in consideration for any speech given, article published, or attendance at any public or private conference, convention, meeting, social gathering, meal, or like gathering."

The *Fair Political Practices Commission* (FPPC) administers and enforces the Political Reform Act. It can investigate charges of violations, subpoena records and witnesses, issue cease and desist orders, and levy fines. The commission is a five-member board, no more than three of whom may be from the same political party. The governor appoints two members from different parties; the attorney general, the secretary of state, and the state controller each appoint one member.

Violations of the Political Reform Act may result in civil or criminal penalties. Private citizens may report violations and bring actions to stop them. Anyone convicted of a misdemeanor under the Political Reform Act may not be a candidate for office or a lobbyist for four years, unless the court rules otherwise at the time of sentencing. The criminal penalty for illegal contributions or improper reporting is a fine of up to $10,000, or three times the amount involved in the violation, whichever is greater. The attorney general enforces the criminal provisions on the state level; city attorneys and district attorneys share responsibility with the attorney general at the local level. The Fair Political Practices Commission, city attorneys, and district attorneys share responsibility for civil prosecutions. The FPPC can also levy administrative fines of up to $2,000.

CALIFORNIA'S POLITICAL PARTIES

A political party is a public organization of citizens working to advance its governmental policies by nominating candidates for office and waging campaigns on their behalf.

PARTY FORMATION

A group or organization may qualify as a political party and have the names of its candidates printed on the official ballot by demonstrating popular support in one of two ways:

- The number of voters registered with that party must equal or exceed one percent of the votes cast in the last gubernatorial election.
- Registered voters equal to ten percent of those voting in the last gubernatorial election must sign a petition declaring that they represent a political party.

  In addition to the Democratic and Republican parties, the American Independent, Green, Libertarian, and Peace & Freedom parties qualified for the 1992 California ballot. Loss of official status means a party's candidates may only receive write-in votes. In order to remain an official party, both of the following conditions must be met:

- One of the party's candidates for statewide office must have received at least two percent of the vote cast for that office in the last gubernatorial election.
- The number of voters registered with that party must be at least one-fifteenth of one percent of the total state registration.

PARTY ORGANIZATION

Anyone who declares a party preference when registering to vote is legally a party member. About 90 percent of California voters belong to a political party. The chief function of these grassroots members is to select their party's nominee in the primary election and support party candidates in the general election. Those who wish a more active role within the party may seek a position on the county or state central committee.

The central committees are the permanent organizations of each party. Their organization and operation, including title, membership, function, selection of officers, and time and place of meetings, are determined by law.

The *county central committee* organizes campaigns for party candidates in the county. Any registered party member may file a petition asking to be nominated to the committee. Members are elected at the primary election for two-year terms; vacancies are usually filled by appointment. In addition to elected members, party incumbents and nominees from that county are members with full privileges, including voting. The membership of the committee ranges in size from 20 to 200, depending on county population and voting patterns.

The *state central committee* conducts campaigning and fundraising on a larger scale than that of the county central committee. State party chairs serve four-year terms and cannot succeed themselves. The chair alternates between northern and southern California. Party membership is very large. For the Republican, Democratic, and American Independent parties, the state central committee includes all party officeholders and nominees at the state level as well as numerous appointees of elected officials and of the county central committees. The Democratic committee is the largest (over 2,800 members), because it includes an additional 400 local representatives chosen at Assembly district caucuses throughout the state. The state central committee of the Libertarian, and Peace & Freedom parties are composed of the members of the county central committee.

UNOFFICIAL PARTY ORGANIZATIONS

Some of the continuous work of the party is done by voluntary political groups which are not a part of the organization and are not bound by the laws governing parties. The groups provide a forum of party members of similar convictions and work to influence their party's policies by supporting candidates who represent their views. Unlike the official parties, they are free to endorse candidates in the primary election, a crucial time for influencing the direction of party policy. Unofficial party organizations which have had a significant influence on politics in California include the California Democratic Council, the Federation of Young Democrats, the California Republican Assembly, the United Republicans of California, and the California Republican League.

4

INITIATIVE AND REFERENDUM

Citizens in a representative democracy rely primarily on their elected representatives to make the laws. However, the people of California reserve to themselves the power to initiate and to annul laws using two forms of direct legislation, the initiative and the referendum.

The initiative process in California gives voters the power to propose a law (statutory initiative) and to propose a change in the state constitution (constitutional amendment initiative). If the required number of voters sign a petition, the initiative proposal is placed on a statewide ballot for approval or rejection. The referendum process gives voters the power to place a measure passed by the legislature on a statewide ballot for voter approval or rejection; such a measure is temporarily suspended, pending a decision by the voters.

Constitutional amendments providing for the initiative and referendum were passed by the state legislature in 1911, along with a long list of additional changes resulting from the Progressive movement. The proposals for direct legislation were approved by a three-to-one margin in a statewide special election that year.

INITIATIVE

California, like most states that allow the initiative, uses the form known as the direct initiative. This process bypasses the legislature completely; a qualified measure is placed directly on the ballot for decision by the voters.

PROCEDURES AND REQUIREMENTS

There are several distinct steps in the initiative process:

Drafting. First citizens write the text of their proposed law or constitutional amendment. The legislative counsel is authorized to assist in the drafting if requested to do so by 25 or more qualified voters. The secretary of state will review a draft for clarity if the proponents ask for such assistance.

Titling. The draft, along with $200, is submitted to the attorney general, whose office prepares a title and summary.

If the measure qualifies for the ballot within two years of the summary date, the money is refunded.

Calculating deadlines. When the secretary of state receives a copy of the title and summary from the attorney general, procedural deadlines are calculated. Proponents have 150 days, or about five months, in which to complete the petition process.

Circulating. Only registered voters are entitled to circulate and sign a petition. Each qualified voter may sign an initiative petition only once.

Filing. The signed petition is filed with the election official of the county in which the signatures were gathered. All sections circulated in a particular county must be filed at the same time. Election officials determine the total number of valid signatures. Since 1976 a random sampling system has been used, which in most instances has eliminated the need to verify every signature.

Qualifying. A greater number of signatures is required to propose a change in the constitution than to propose a change in a law or statute. A constitutional initiative qualifies for the ballot if petitions are signed by registered voters equal in number to eight percent of the votes cast for all gubernatorial candidates in the last such election. The number needed for the November 1992 ballot was 615,958.

A statutory initiative qualifies for the ballot if petitions are signed by registered voters equal in number to five percent of the votes cast for all gubernatorial candidates in the last such election. The total number of signatures required for the November 1992 ballot was 384,974.

Campaigning. The secretary of state sends copies of the qualified initiative to the legislature. Though the legislature has no authority to alter the measure or prevent it from going to the ballot, joint public hearings are required, but not always held. Arguments for and against the initiative are printed in the ballot pamphlet that is mailed to all voter households.

Under the Political Reform Act of 1974, proponents must file campaign statements. There are no restrictions on the amounts of money that can be contributed or spent in support of or opposition to statewide initiative measures. Campaign committees must, however, file financial disclosure statements. The Fair Political Practices Commission regularly reports this information to the public.

Voting. An initiative passes if it is approved by a majority of those voting on the measure. Once adopted by the initiative process, a law can be changed only by the same process, unless the initiative statute itself contains a specific provision allowing the legislature to amend it.

USE OF INITIATIVES

The state constitution limits an initiative to only one subject. The California Supreme Court has held that a measure meets the single subject test if all of its parts are "reasonably germane."

An initiative may not name a person to office. Neither may the process be used to assign a duty or power to a particular private corporation.

The initiative process in California has been used by a wide variety of interest groups. Early ballot measures frequently dealt with moral and economic issues. Later initiatives turned more to questions of administrative organization, such as the creation of licensing boards for chiropractors and osteopaths. Initiatives of the 1920's and 1930's addressed civil service, judicial reform, and the executive budget. Old-age pension measures appeared on the ballot from the 1930's to the 1950's. Public school funding was a major topic of initiatives in the 1940's and the 1950's.

Civil rights issues came to the forefront in the 1960's. The decade of the 1970's brought environmental issues to the ballot, as well as a series of initiatives to cut taxes. The Jarvis-Gann initiative to limit property taxes, the most widely known of the tax reform initiatives, appeared as Proposition 13 on the 1978 primary election ballot.

The predominant issues of the early 1980's included taxation, campaign contribution limits, public aid programs, handgun control and a state lottery. The latter is an example of an issue that was the subject of many unsuccessful initiative attempts before finally winning voter approval. In 1986 voters passed Proposition 65, the Safe Drinking Water and Toxics Enforcement Act. Voters in 1988 narrowly approved a constitutional amendment on education, Proposition 98. Insurance reform, AIDS measures, and an increase in the state's tobacco tax were among some of the major issues on the ballot in the late 1980's. The initiatives of 1990 contained such important issues as improved transportation funding, redistricting, environmental protection, and legislative term limits.

Senate apportionment was the subject of initiatives in 1948, 1960, 1962, 1982, and 1990. In November 1982 and June 1990, initiative proposals to turn reapportionment responsibilities over to an independent commission were rejected by the voters. An initiative redrawing legislative district lines qualified for the ballot in 1983. However, the state Supreme Court ruled it off the ballot, stating that the constitution permits redistricting only once per decade.

According to secretary of state records, 765 direct initiatives were circulated between 1912 general election and the 1992 primary election. Of that total, 229 actually qualified for the ballot. Three of those were ruled off the ballot as unconstitutional. Of the 226 appearing on the ballot, voters approved and passed a total of 72.

The highest number of initiatives on a single ballot was 17 in 1914, six of which won approval. In recent years the greatest number of initiatives facing the voters was 13 in November 1990.

Although there has been an upsurge in the number of initiative petitions circulated in recent years, the number qualifying and passing is not as dramatic, as indicated in **Figure 4.1.**

INITIATIVES IN CALIFORNIA

Year	# Circulated	# Qualified	# Approved
1972	23	10	3
1973	6	1	0
1974	33	2	1
1976	35	3	0
1978	26	4	2
1980	59	5	1
1982	66	9	5
1983	14	2	1
1984	31	7	2
1986	34	6	4
1988	63	18	9
1990	66	18	6
1992*	35	0	0

* as of June primary election

Figure 4.1

PROPOSALS FOR CHANGE

Most proposals to change the initiative process center on the necessity for court action, the role of money, a lack of substantive information for voters, and the role of legislators.

Some suggest that drafting could be improved if each initiative measure had to be reviewed by an official authority for clarity. Some seek further definition of the single subject rule. Others propose to change the number of signatures necessary to qualify, require a certain geographic distribution of signatures, change the time allowed to collect signatures, or forbid paying those who solicit signatures.

Various limitations have been suggested for the campaign stage. These include the amount an individual or group can contribute, requiring more complete disclosure of contributors, providing public financing for initiative campaigns, providing more public hearings, and writing simpler analyses in the voter pamphlet.

Prior to 1966 proponents could pursue either the direct or the indirect initiative route. Under the indirect form, the proposal was submitted first to the legislature. The legislature had 40 days to enact or reject the proposal. If the legislature adopted it without change, it became law. If the legislature rejected it or failed to act, the initiative then went on to the ballot for decision by the people. This indirect procedure was used so infrequently that it was repealed in 1966. Yet interest in this form of the initiative continues to be expressed. Nearly every legislative session since 1985 has included attempts to reinstate the indirect initiative process.

REFERENDUM

California is one of twenty-four states which uses the petition form of referendum. Using petition reform, voters can demand that a measure enacted by the legislature and signed by the governor be referred to the electorate before going into effect.

PROCEDURES AND REQUIREMENTS

Most states providing the referendum put some restrictions on its use. California does not permit use of this procedure to challenge statutes which call elections or provide for tax levies or appropriations for current expenses. Any other law is subject to the referendum unless it is enacted as an urgency statute.

The state constitution defines an urgency statute as one "necessary for the immediate preservation of the public peace, health, or safety." An urgency statute passes the legislature only if it is approved by a two-thirds vote in each house; it cannot be referred to the voters through the referendum process.

The referendum process can be described in several stages:

Titling. Before circulating a referendum petition, proponents must submit it to the attorney general for a title and summary.

Circulating. Referendum proponents have 90 days to complete the entire process of circulating petitions and verifying that the required number of valid signatures has been submitted. The three-month period begins the day a bill is enacted.

Qualifying. A petition referendum qualifies for the ballot if it is signed by voters equal in number to five percent of those who cast votes in the governor's race in the most recent gubernatorial election. The total number of signatures required for the November 1992 election was 384,974.

Voting. The law or section of the law that is challenged takes effect only if it is approved by a majority of those voting on the question in the next election. The governor is permitted to call a special election for consideration of a referendum. The legislature is permitted to amend or repeal referendum statutes.

USE OF REFERENDUMS

Fewer subjects have been addressed by referendum than by initiative. Measures dealing with oil production, drilling on tidelands owned by the state, and taxation on oleomargarine were among the early topics.

Reapportionment has been the subject of direct legislation more than once. The district lines by the legislature in 1928 were sustained in a referendum. In a June 1982 referendum vote the people of the state rejected the district lines drawn by the legislature. Subsequently, the legislature adopted a replacement set of lines.

A total of thirty-nine referendums by petition have appeared on

California ballots since 1912. The voters have overturned the legislature's actions on twenty-five occasions, or in 64 percent of the cases.

Legislative decisions were challenged and referred to the voters with the greatest frequency during the 1920's and 1930's. In 1952, a measure dealing with tax exemptions of nonprofit schools was approved in a referendum vote in a close decision. The referendum then fell into a period of disuse for almost thirty years.

In June 1982, two issues reached the ballot by the referendum process. That year the legislature had passed measures addressing district reapportionment and construction of state water facilities. The voters rejected the legislature's plan in both instances.

LOCAL DIRECT LEGISLATION

The people of California also are constitutionally guaranteed the use of the initiative and referendum at local government level. These forms of direct legislation have been used more often in cities than in counties.

Charter cities establish their own procedures. General law cities and counties operate under provisions of the state elections code. In these jurisdictions proponents submit a proposal to the city or county clerk, whichever is appropriate. They must publish a notice of intent to circulate an initiative petition.

The time period allowed for gathering signatures is more generous at the local level than at the state level. Petition circulators have 180 days to qualify a local initiative or referendum, as opposed to 150 days to qualify a statewide initiative and 90 days to qualify a statewide referendum.

At the municipal level the total signatures required is based on a percentage of the city's registered voters. The signature requirements at the county level are based on the number of votes cast within that county for candidates for governor in the last election.

A completed initiative petition is presented to the appropriate elected body, either the city council or the board of supervisors. The elected body may adopt the proposal without change, thereby ending the process. If the council or board refuses to act or wishes to make changes, the proposition is submitted to the voters at the next regular election. If the petitions are signed by a large number of voters, the council or board must call a special election to decide the issue.

SEPARATING THE POWERS

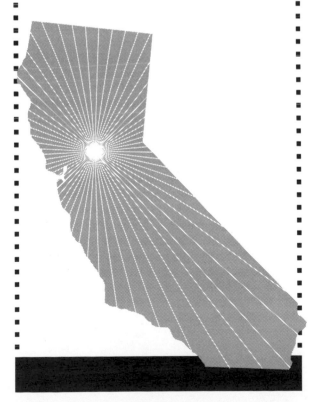

5

LEGISLATIVE BRANCH

The state constitution separates the powers of state government into three main branches: legislative, executive, and judicial. The legislative branch has the authority to make laws; the executive branch, to administer laws; the judicial branch, to interpret laws and ensure that they are applied justly and equitably.

The system of checks and balances provided in the constitution results in certain exceptions to these normally distinct roles. For example, the governor, as chief executive of the state, has the authority to veto legislation; legislators are constitutionally authorized to serve on certain administrative boards in the executive branch.

LEGISLATIVE POWERS

The principal lawmaking powers of the state are vested in the legislature. Every year the legislature adopts thousands of new laws or changes in the law, in response to new situations and needs.

The subject matter of state laws is limited only by certain federal restrictions. When state and federal laws conflict or cover the same subject, federal laws often prevail, although California imposes stricter standards on environmental issues and firearms possession, for example. The U.S. Supreme Court has extended federal jurisdiction into areas such as civil and criminal rights, primarily on the basis of the Bill of Rights and the Fourteenth Amendment, which declares:

> *No state shall make or enforce any law which shall abridge the privileges or immunities of citizens of the United States; nor shall any State deprive any person of life, liberty, or property without due process of law; nor deny to any person within its jurisdiction the equal protection of the laws.*

The legislature has broad power over local governments. Counties, cities, regional agencies, and special districts may be created only in accordance with state law. When local ordinances and state laws conflict or cover the same subject, state laws generally prevail.

The legislature controls public finances by levying taxes and appropriating funds. (**See Chapter 18, Budget and Finance.**)

As part of the system of checks and balances, the legislature has statutory influence over the funding, organization, and procedures used by administrative agencies of the executive branch. It also has the authority to appoint citizens to policy-making committees in the executive branch and to designate members of the legislature to serve on agency boards. Many appointments made by the governor are subject to legislative approval.

The legislature's role in the impeachment process serves as a check on both the executive and judicial branches. The state Assembly has the power to impeach; that is, to accuse an elected state official or judge of misconduct in office; the Senate tries impeachment cases.

THE LEGISLATORS

The federal government and all states except Nebraska have a bicameral legislature, a legislature divided into two houses; in California these are the state Senate and the state Assembly. Legislators are elected by district, one member from each district. The districts are contiguous and are numbered consecutively, beginning in the north and ending in the south. The constitution calls for 40 Senate districts and 80 Assembly districts. In 1992, each Senate district represented an average of 750,000 constituents, while each Assembly district represented an average of 375,000 constituents. Detailed maps of district boundaries are available from legislators' offices and from the elections division of the secretary of state's office.

REAPPORTIONMENT AND REDISTRICTING

Districts of a particular type (e.g. Senate) must be reasonably equal in population. Consequently, a district in a rural, sparsely populated area is much larger, geographically, than one in an urban, densely populated area. The lines of the districts are adjusted after each national census to reflect changes in the population. The census is taken at the beginning of each decade; the state constitution requires the legislature to adjust district boundary lines in the following year.

The legislature is responsible for redistricting state Senate and Assembly, U.S. Congressional, and Board of Equalization districts. The governor must sign the legislative plan for its approval; if vetoed, the legislature may attempt an override with a two-thirds vote. Failing a two-thirds vote, the matter may be decided by the Supreme Court.

From 1982 to 1992 five ballot initiatives proposing change in the redistricting process were rejected by the voters.

In 1991, the redistricting process was sent to the state Supreme Court as a result of the governor's refusal to enact any legislative redistricting proposals. In January 1992, a panel of special masters comprised of retired justices appointed by the Supreme Court presented new district lines and re-drew the boundaries for all legislative and congressional districts.

Shifting the previous boundaries changed the dynamics of California's political landscape, leaving many legislators without districts. Incumbent state lawmakers were forced to decide whether to run in their new, more competitively shaped districts, run for another elected position, campaign for one of the seven new congressional seats gained in the most recent census, or retire from public office altogether.

ELIGIBILITY AND ELECTION

Any U.S. citizen 18 years of age or older who has been a California resident for three years and a resident of a legislative district for one year immediately preceding an election is eligible to hold legislative office. Legislators are elected on a partisan ballot.

With the appearance of term limits **(see Figure 5.1, About Proposition 140)** on the political landscape, state senators may serve only two four-year terms; Assembly members may serve only three two-year terms. All 80 Assembly seats and half of the 40 Senate seats are up for election every even-numbered year. A vacancy in either house is generally filled by special election announced by the governor.

The constitution gives each house of the legislature the power to judge the qualifications and elections of its members and to expel one of its members by a two-thirds vote. Legislators are bound by a code of ethics, adopted in 1966, dealing with conflict of interest; complaints are handled by the Joint Legislative Ethics Committee. There is also a Senate Committee on Legislative Ethics, which enforces Standards of Conduct in the Senate. Finally, members of the legislature are subject to the provisions of the Political Reform Act of 1974.

COMPENSATION

The California legislature is almost a full-time body. Lawmakers receive an annual salary and reimbursement on a per diem, or per day, basis for travel and living expenses in connection with their official duties. The salary levels are set by the California Citizens Compensation Commission. The independent commission was created by the passage of Proposition 112 in 1990. Proposition 112 also banned elected officials from accepting honoraria (i.e., speaking fees), limited the value of gifts they can receive from special interests, and prohibited them from lobbying their former colleagues for a year after leaving office.

In 1991, the commission established the annual income for all elective members in state government. In 1992, the annual salary for a state legislator was $52,500; majority and minority floor leaders each receive $57,750, and, the speaker of the Assembly and the Senate president pro tempore each receive $63,000.

The State Board of Control sets the level of per diem paid to the legislature. In 1992, the per diem allowance for living expenses while on legislative business was raised from $92 to $100 per day. A legislator is eligible for living expenses for each day spent on state business in

Sacramento. A specific request must be made for living expenses for official time spent outside of Sacramento.

Each legislator also receives $5,400 or 90 percent, whichever is less, towards a state-leased automobile, allowances for postage, expenses in district offices, and mileage on personal cars. The state pays commercial transportation costs and expenses for cars owned or leased by the state.

The retirement system for legislators is supported partly by member contributions and partly by the General Fund. A former legislator is eligible for a full pension after 21 years of service or at age 60. The pension may not exceed two-thirds of the lawmaker's salary at the time of retirement, except for annual cost-of-living adjustments.

SENATE LEADERSHIP

The *lieutenant governor* is designated by the constitution as president of the Senate, largely a ceremonial post. This officer has no role in the routine business of the Senate and votes only when there is a tie and one more vote would provide the necessary vote needed to approve a motion or measure. (In 1982, the voters rejected a plan to remove the lieutenant governor as president of the Senate.)

The *president pro tempore* is responsible for the overall administration of the Senate. Elected by the Senate, the pro tem chairs the Senate Rules Committee, promotes the prompt disposition of bills and other business before the Senate.

The *Senate Rules Committee,* chaired by the president pro tempore, is composed of four other members elected by the state Senate. This committee has the power to appoint all other Senate committees, designate chairs and vice chairs of standing committees, and decide which committee will consider each bill. The committee also makes recommendations on the confirmation of many gubernatorial appointments.

The rules committee decides which senators will serve on executive and judicial boards and commissions. All expenditures and claims for reimbursement by Senate committees must be approved by this committee.

Majority and minority floor leaders are chosen by their respective party caucuses to manage political strategy. The majority and minority party caucuses also elect their own chairs to lead party policy meetings.

ASSEMBLY LEADERSHIP

The *speaker of the Assembly,* the presiding officer of that body, is elected from and by the Assembly membership and serves ex-officio on all Assembly and joint legislative committees.

The power of the Assembly speaker is broader than that of the pro tem of the Senate. The speaker names the majority floor leader and the chair of the rules committee; assists in establishing the size and membership of all standing committees; designates the chairs and vice chairs of policy committees, who must be from opposite political parties; and selects members for executive and judicial boards and commissions.

The *speaker pro tempore* is elected by the Assembly to perform leadership duties during the speaker's absence. The speaker pro tem is an ex-officio member of the rules committee with no vote.

The *Assembly Rules Committee* is chaired by the speaker or the speaker's appointee. The majority and minority caucuses each nominate four additional members; the eight nominees must be approved by majority vote of the Assembly. The rules committee refers bills to committees, and selects and supervises Assembly support staff. It is responsible for expediting procedures and proposing changes in house rules. Members of this committee may not chair standing committees.

The *floor leader* of the majority party is appointed by the Assembly speaker; the minority floor leader is chosen by the minority caucus. The majority and minority caucus chairs are chosen by their respective parties.

LEGISLATIVE COMMITTEES

Policy committees are standing committees established in the rules adopted by each house; their membership usually changes after each election. Some establish subcommittees to facilitate their work. Each committee is assigned bills in its subject area to hear, study, and vote on.

Committee names change slightly from session to session, but each house has committees which deal with similar issue areas. Areas addressed include: agriculture and water resources, banking, commerce, and international trade, business and professions, consumer protection, constitutional amendments, education, elections, energy, environmental safety, government organization, health and human services, housing, insurance, industrial relations, judiciary, labor, local government, natural resources, public employees and retirement, public safety, revenue and taxation, transportation, utilities and commerce, veterans affairs, water, parks, and wildlife.

In the interim period between legislative sessions, committees can meet to gather information and make recommendations, though they may not take official actions. Interim hearings are sometimes held outside Sacramento to permit testimony by experts and residents in different parts of the state.

Fiscal committees are standing committees that handle the annual state budget and all other bills with either a direct or implied cost to the state. Bills with fiscal implications, often the most important bills, are referred to fiscal committees from policy committees.

Special or select committees may be set up by either house to research a comparatively limited subject, such as child abuse or mobile homes.

Joint committees include members of both houses, appointed by the speaker in the Assembly and by the rules committee in the Senate. Such committees can conduct investigations, hold hearings, and recommend legislation.

Conference committees, set up to resolve differences in the Assembly and Senate versions of bills, are composed of three members of each house, chosen by the Assembly speaker and the Senate Rules Committee.

LEGISLATIVE STAFF

Although California has one of the largest legislative staffs in the nation, it was substantially reduced by Proposition 140. Support staff provide legal, technical, research, and secretarial services for the legislators. Most employees of the legislature are appointed by the rules committee in each house and are exempt from civil service.

ABOUT PROPOSITION 140

Proposition 140 added new provisions to the California Constitution by placing limits on the terms of office served by state officials, requiring major cuts in the operating budget of the legislature, and setting a limit on all future legislative operating budgets. A provision prohibiting further state contributions to any retirement system for legislators other than federal Social Security was dismissed by the state Supreme Court in a legislative challenge to the law. Voters passed Proposition 140 by a majority of 52 to 48 percent on the November 1990 ballot.

Summary of Proposition 140's key provisions:

- Limits state senators to two four-year terms.

- Limits Assembly members to three two-year terms.

- Limits elected executive officers including the governor, lieutenant governor, secretary of state, treasurer, controller, attorney general, and members of the Board of Equalization to two four-year terms in the same office.

- Cut the legislature's operating budget by 38 percent.

- Would have required state legislators to participate in the federal Social Security program and terminate any future contributions for pension and retirement benefits. However, the state Supreme Court overturned this provision in 1991.

Figure 5.1

Each member of the legislature is entitled to an administrative assistant and secretaries for both district and capitol offices. Additional personnel are provided for larger districts or workloads.

Each committee chair is provided one or more committee consultants, depending on the workload of the particular committee. Especially knowledgeable in their subject areas, committee consultants analyze bills, help draft legislation, plan hearings, and conduct studies.

Offices of research provide services for each house. The majority and minority party caucuses in each house are assisted by consultants.

The chief legal advisor to the legislature is the *legislative counsel*. A nonpartisan position, the legislative counsel is elected at the beginning of each regular session by both houses. Although the legislative counsel provides legal services which the legislature may desire in connection with their legislative activities, a greater portion of their work is concerned with legislative issues. The legislative counsel's office prepares bills, resolutions, and amendments according to the requests of the legislators; advises legislators on the constitutionality and legality of proposed measures; and prepares digests and indexes of codes and statutes.

Fiscal advice is provided by the *legislative analyst*. A nonpartisan position, the legislative analyst is appointed by the Joint Legislative Budget Committee. The analyst's staff evaluates the proposed state budget, revenues and expenditures; makes fiscal analyses of each bill assigned to a fiscal committee; and responds to legislative requests for information. The legislative analyst also prepares an analysis of each proposition for the state ballot pamphlet.

The *auditor general* assists the legislature by evaluating the performance of state and local programs as the state's watchdog. A nonpartisan position, the auditor general is appointed by a concurrent resolution of the legislature. The auditor general also annually performs a financial audit of California as required by the federal government.

Since Proposition 140 cut the legislature's operating budget, the offices of the auditor general and legislative analyst were in danger of being unfunded. While legislation was introduced in 1992 to establish the auditor general and legislative analyst as constitutional offices with their own budgets, voters will have to decide these issues on the June 1992 ballot.

LEGISLATIVE PROCEDURES

The state constitution defines specific dates on which, and number of days in which, the legislature must complete certain procedures. Within this framework, each house determines its own standing rules of procedure.

Each session is convened under the standing rules of the previous session. Each house then adopts the same or new rules to govern procedural matters such as the committee system, duties of officers, order of daily business, parliamentary rules, and joint legislative rules, for the new session.

LEGISLATIVE SESSIONS

The governor is constitutionally authorized to call the legislature into special session at any time to deal with urgent or extraordinary issues. Action during a special session is limited to the subjects specified by the governor. Procedural rules permit speedier action during a special session than a regular session. Laws passed in special session take effect 91 days after the session adjourns.

The new legislature convenes each two-year session in December after each general election. A regular session lasts two years; the meeting schedule is as follows:

	Even-numbered years
December	New legislative session begins

	Odd-numbered years
January	Regular session begins
Spring	One-week recess
Summer	One-month recess
September-December	Interim study recess

	Even-numbered years
January	Regular session resumes
Spring	One-week recess
Summer	One-month recess
August 31	End of regular session
November 30	Adjournment

TYPES OF LEGISLATION

A *bill* is a proposal to change, repeal, or add to existing state law. An Assembly bill (AB) is one introduced in the Assembly; a Senate bill (SB), in the Senate. Bills are designated by number, in the order of introduction in each house. For example, AB 16 refers to the sixteenth bill introduced in the Assembly. The numbering starts afresh each session.

The legislature takes other kinds of action by resolution, though the term *bill* is often used loosely to include resolutions.

A *constitutional amendment,* known as an ACA or SCA, depending on the house of origin, is a resolution proposing a change in the constitution. An ACA or SCA must be approved by two-thirds of the members of each house by a certain deadline in order to qualify for a statewide ballot. A constitutional amendment must be approved by a majority of voters to take effect.

A *concurrent resolution* is used to adopt joint rules, establish joint committees, commend persons or organizations, or express legislative intent. Referred to as an ACR or SCR, depending on the house of origin, a concurrent resolution needs only a majority vote of each house to pass.

A *joint resolution,* referred to as an AJR or SJR, depending on the house of origin, usually urges passage or defeat of legislation pending before the U.S. Congress or urges presidential action.

A *house resolution* expresses the sentiment of either the Assembly (AR) or Senate (SR). A house resolution is used, for example, to create an interim committee, amend a house rule, or congratulate an individual or group; it is usually adopted by majority voice vote.

LEGISLATIVE PROCESS

The legislature handles bills according to a process prescribed by the constitution and statutory law to ensure opportunity for citizen input. The requirements and deadlines that are part of the bill process do not apply to resolutions or the budget bill. (**See Chapter 18, Budget and Finance.**)

The legislative process, outlined in **Figure 5.2**, is divided into distinct stages:

Drafting. Upon the request of a legislator, the legislative counsel's office drafts the formal language of a bill and a digest of its main provisions. Ideas for proposals often come from various organizations and individuals, such as legislative committees, the executive branch, counties, cities, businesses, lobbyists, and citizens.

Introduction. A bill can be introduced in either house of the legislature, at which time it is numbered and read for the first time. (The constitution requires, with limited exception, that a bill be read by title on three separate days in each house.) The name of the author, the legislator who introduced the bill, becomes part of the title. The bill is printed and subject to a 30-day waiting period before it can be heard or acted upon.

Policy committee. The rules committee of the house of origin assigns each bill to a policy committee appropriate to the subject matter. The committee hears public testimony from the author, proponents, and opponents. The committee can take no action, pass the original or an amended form of the bill, kill it by holding it in committee, refer it to another committee, amend it and re-refer it to itself, or send it to interim study. Approval of a bill requires a majority of those on the committee.

Fiscal committee. If approved by the policy committee, a bill which contains an appropriation or has financial implications for the state is sent to the fiscal committee, where similar consideration and actions can occur. Approval of a bill requires a majority of those on the committee.

Second reading. A bill recommended for passage by committee is read a second time on the floor of the house. Ordinarily there is little or no debate. If a bill is amended at this stage, it may be referred back for another committee hearing.

Floor vote. A bill is read a third time, debated, and possibly amended on the floor. A roll call vote is taken. An ordinary bill needs a majority vote to pass (21 votes in the Senate, 41 votes in the Assembly). An urgency bill or a bill with fiscal implications requires a two-thirds vote (27 votes in the Senate, 54 in the Assembly).

Second house. If it receives a favorable vote in the first house, a bill repeats the same steps in the other house. If the second house passes the bill without changing it, it is sent to the governor's desk.

Concurrence or conference. If a measure is amended in the second house and passed, it is returned to the house of origin for consideration of amendments. The house of origin may concur with the amendments and send the bill to the governor or reject the amendments and submit it to a two-house conference committee. If either house rejects the conference report, a second (and even a third) conference committee can be formed. If both houses adopt the conference report, the bill is sent to the governor.

Governor's action. Within 12 days after receiving a bill, the governor may sign it into law, allow it to become law without a signature, or veto it. In bills that appropriate funds, the governor may veto or reduce particular expenditure items while approving the rest of the provisions. When the legislature recesses in mid-September of an odd-numbered year, the governor has until mid-October to make decisions on bills. When the legislature concludes its work in August of an even-numbered year, the governor has until September 30th to make decisions on bills.

Overrides. A vetoed bill is returned to the house of origin, where a vote may be taken to override the governor's veto; a two-thirds vote of both houses is required to override a veto.

Effective date. Ordinarily a law passed during a regular session takes effect January 1 of the following year. A few statutes go into effect as soon as the governor signs them; these include acts calling for elections and urgency measures necessary for the immediate preservation of the public peace, health, or safety.

TRACKING LEGISLATION

About 5,000 pieces of legislation are introduced during each two-year session. Each house publishes three guides during the session to assist those trying to keep track of the bills.

The *Daily File* for each house is an agenda of the day's business. It lists measures scheduled for committee hearing and house action, the location and meeting time of each committee, and the current membership of all standing committees. A visitor to the capitol may obtain this publication in the bill room.

The *Daily Journal* contains an account of the proceedings of each house for the preceding day. It includes the titles of all measures introduced, considered, or acted upon; the text of house resolutions,

TYPICAL PATH OF LEGISLATION

SUGGESTIONS FOR LEGISLATION
from a variety of sources

LEGISLATION DRAFTED
ASSEMBLY ——— by legislative counsel ——— SENATE
at legislator's request

ASSEMBLY	SENATE
BILL INTRODUCED first reading	**BILL INTRODUCED** first reading
ASSIGNED TO COMMITTEE by rules committee	**ASSIGNED TO COMMITTEE** by rules committee
POLICY COMMITTEE HEARING public testimony	**POLICY COMMITTEE HEARING** public testimony
fail — pass	pass — fail
FISCAL COMMITTEE HEARING public testimony	**FISCAL COMMITTEE HEARING** public testimony
fail — pass	pass — fail
ASSEMBLY FLOOR second reading	**SENATE FLOOR** second reading
FLOOR DEBATE AND VOTE third reading	**FLOOR DEBATE AND VOTE** third reading
fail — pass	pass — fail
TO SENATE process repeated	**TO ASSEMBLY** process repeated

PASSED SECOND HOUSE
without change

or

CONCURRENCE
with amendments

or

CONFERENCE COMMITTEE
to resolve differences

——— **TO GOVERNOR** ———

SIGNED INTO LAW   **BECOMES LAW WITHOUT SIGNATURE**   **VETOED**

OVERRIDE POSSIBLE
by legislature

Figure 5.2

roll calls, messages from the governor and the other house; and committee reports, motions, and roll calls. Senate committee votes are reported in the Senate's *Journal;* Assembly committee votes, in a separate appendix to the Assembly's *Journal.* No record is kept of arguments in debate.

A *History* is published by each house. The *Weekly History*, published at the end of each week, summarizes all action taken on every measure from the beginning of the session through the end of that week. Each chamber's *Daily History* shows the action taken on the action file each day since the last *Weekly History*. A *Semifinal History* is issued by the Assembly in February following the first year of the session. When the legislature adjourns, a *Final History* is published, summarizing all legislation introduced and acted upon during the two-year session.

The *Index*, published by the legislative counsel, is used to access various pieces of legislation by either house by subject matter.

Single copies of the daily and weekly publications and of individual bills are available free from the legislative bill room in the capitol; each request must specify the bill number and session of origin. County law libraries and many public libraries maintain complete sets of bills while the legislature is in session. Additionally, brochures and pamphlets on state government and the legislature are provided by the bill room, members of the legislature, the chief clerk of the Assembly, and the secretary of the Senate.

PUBLIC INPUT

Legislators enact laws on behalf of the people of the state. Californians have the right to express their views on proposed measures as individuals, in cooperation with others, and through legislative advocates. Public support or opposition to a bill or budget item can be expressed in many ways: timely letters to legislative representatives, testimony before committees, personal visits to legislative officials, and public information campaigns, to name a few.

Some issue-oriented organizations hire advocates or lobbyists to help them communicate their views on legislative and administrative matters directly to elected officials and agencies. In 1991, 856 professional lobbyists (or legislative advocates as they prefer to be called) were registered with 276 firms representing a variety of businesses, utilities, professional associations, cities, counties, labor unions, environmental organizations, and public interest groups.

The Political Reform Act of 1974 regulates the activities of lobbyists; for instance, lobbyists must register with the secretary of state each legislative session; file quarterly reports of bills lobbied, expenses incurred, and payments received; and limit the value of gifts to any legislator to $10 per month.

6

EXECUTIVE BRANCH

The California Constitution declares, "The supreme executive power of this State is vested in the Governor. The Governor shall see that the law is faithfully executed." Under the leadership of the governor, many thousands of persons work in the executive branch, handling a wide range of governmental responsibilities. Although the state's highest eight executive officers are directly elected by the people, many other high-ranking state officers are appointed by the governor. The vast majority of positions in the executive branch, however, are covered by the state's civil service system.

ROLE OF THE EXECUTIVE BRANCH

While the usual explanation of responsibilities of the branches of government is that the legislature makes the laws and the executive branch administers and enforces them, in practice the legislative and executive branches often work together on shaping proposed legislation. This is true partially because a plan is likely to come to fruition only with the cooperation and consent of both branches, but also because experience of the executive branch in implementing past legislation and coping with new problems provides legislators with information and ideas not available elsewhere.

Many program ideas originate within the agencies and departments of the executive branch. Though a final decision may be made by the department director, agency secretary, or the governor, staff usually prepare information and position papers, and in many cases the higher official need only approve or disapprove.

If legislation is required, procedures established by the governor's office are followed before the legislative counsel is requested to draft a bill or a legislator is asked to sponsor it. Any proposal which involves appropriation, federal funds, or future costs must be reviewed by the Department of Finance. In case of significant impacts the governor may confer with legislators, department heads, agency secretaries, and others while the proposal is being formulated.

On request, departments also aid legislators in preparation or review of proposed legislation. At a later stage administrators may furnish further information or testify before legislative committees.

Many laws are broadly drawn, delegating to the executive units the power and responsibility of working out details as needed through administrative decisions and regulations. In practice, implementation of new laws often requires additional or more specific legislation.

ELECTED STATE OFFICERS

All elective officers in the executive branch serve four-year terms beginning the Monday after January 1 following their election. With the passage of Proposition 140 in 1990, all elective officers, except the Insurance Commissioner, are prohibited from serving more than two terms in the same office. All are subject to recall and impeachment. The governor fills vacancies by appointment unless the law provides otherwise. In the event of death, resignation, removal, or disability of the governor, the order of succession is: lieutenant governor, president pro tempore of the Senate, speaker of the Assembly, secretary of state, attorney general, treasurer, and controller. If there is a question of the governor's disability, a commission established by law is authorized to petition the supreme court to make a determination.

THE GOVERNOR

The constitution requires that a candidate for governor be a citizen of the United States, qualified to vote, and a resident of California for at least five years immediately preceding the election. Besides being the highest-ranking executive of the state, the governor is a legislative leader, the commander-in-chief of the state militia, an appointive power in the judicial system, the leader of his or her political party, and ceremonial head of state. In 1992, the annual salary for the governor was $120,000.

As *chief executive*, the governor has extensive financial control, broad powers of appointment, and authority over the entire organization and administration of the executive branch. The governor may propose to group, consolidate, or coordinate agencies and functions. A reorganization proposal has the effect of law 60 days after it is submitted to the legislature or at a date stipulated in the plan, unless either house takes negative action. At the governor's request, executive officers and agencies are required to report on their operations. With ready access to the public, the governor has extensive opportunity to focus attention on operations or proposals and to influence public opinion. Among other substantial subsidiary powers, the governor is president of the board of regents of the University of California and the board of trustees of the California State University.

As *appointing authority*, the governor has the power to make about 2,000 appointments, including almost all state department heads and officials in key policy-making positions, except for constitutional officers. The governor also appoints several hundred members of boards and commissions. In addition, the governor fills unexpired terms of U.S. senators, supervisors in general law counties, and statewide officers when these positions have become vacant through resignation, removal, or death.

A governor can appoint lawyers to fill judicial vacancies at the municipal and superior court level as he or she desires. For the court of appeals and supreme court, gubernatorial nominees must be confirmed by the Commission on Judicial Appointments and subsequently by the electorate at the first regular election thereafter. Since judges may remain in place for years after a governor has left office, these appointments can influence state policy well beyond the term of the appointing executive.

While gubernatorial powers of appointment are significant in shaping state government, in comparison with other states California limits the governor's patronage both in number of positions to be filled and in the practice of making certain appointments. Some restrictions are imposed by law on the governor's powers. A majority vote of both the state Senate and the Assembly is required to approve special gubernatorial appointments to fill vacancies among the constitutional officers. About 170 other appointments require confirmation by the state Senate. Then too, composition of boards may be stipulated in law—for instance, the number of professionals from the field and the number of public representatives. Removal powers are also limited.

Constitutional and statutory law fix the terms of office of some department heads and of many boards and commissions. Terms may be staggered so that a governor cannot appoint a majority of a board, and sometimes terms of appointees are prescribed to be longer than the governor's own term. However, most department heads, the governor's staff, and members of the cabinet serve at the governor's pleasure.

As *legislative leader*, the governor advises the legislature at the beginning of each legislative session as to the condition of the state, recommends legislation, and confers regularly with representatives of the Senate and the Assembly. The governor's office prepares and submits to the legislature the annual state budget covering expenditures for every branch of state government. After legislative adjustment of the budget, the governor may reduce or eliminate particular items by veto, but may not raise them.

The governor may also veto bills passed by the legislature, and the threat of veto may influence legislation (although recent governors have vetoed only about seven percent of all bills passed). The gubernatorial veto is difficult to override, requiring a two-thirds vote in each house; since 1946 only seven attempts to override a governor's veto have succeeded.

The governor may also call a special session of the legislature to consider a specific issue such as a fiscal crisis.

As *commander-in-chief* of the state militia (California National Guard), the governor may call the guard to active duty on his own initiative or on request of local officials in the event of civil disturbance or emergency, including natural disaster.

The governor *influences the judicial system*, by nominating judges to the two highest courts of the state and filling vacancies by appointment in all except justice courts. The governor also has the power to pardon, reprieve, and commute sentences except in cases of impeachment. These clemency powers have few restraints, but the governor's reasons for clemency actions must be reported to the legislature.

As *leader of a political party*, the governor draws strength from party support and exercises influence over party policies and nominations.

As *ceremonial head of state*, the governor performs such duties as ribbon-cutting at public openings and appearing at parades and other celebrations. Though these may seem relatively trivial and time-consuming functions, they can be used by a governor to help build citizen morale and shape public opinion.

OTHER ELECTED EXECUTIVE OFFICERS

The *lieutenant governor* assumes the office of chief executive when the governor is absent from the state or is temporarily or permanently unable to discharge the duties of the office. The lieutenant governor is presiding officer of the Senate and may cast a tie-breaking vote on legislation. He or she may represent the governor as chief of state or be designated to perform executive tasks. The lieutenant governor chairs the Commission on Economic Development and also serves ex-officio on certain boards and commissions such as the State Lands Commission, the board of regents of the University of California, and the board of trustees of the California State University. In 1992, the annual salary for the lieutenant governor was $90,000.

The *secretary of state* is the state's chief elections officer and records keeper. The secretary certifies the nomination and election of candidates; checks for the proper number of signatures for initiative, referendum, and recall petitions; prints the state ballot pamphlets; compiles reports of registration and official statements of the vote; files campaign disclosure and lobbyist financial reports; and enforces elections laws uniformly statewide.

Other major duties of the secretary include the filings of articles of incorporation, limited partnerships, and related corporate documents; registration trademarks; registration of deeds to state lands; filing uniform commercial code division documents such as liens against personal property, tax liens, and judgements; and commissioning of notaries public.

The secretary is also responsible for the California State Archives, which collects, catalogs, indexes and preserves historically valuable papers and artifacts from state government. The secretary maintains the records of acts of the legislature and of the executive branch, and also files all administrative regulations.

As keeper of the state seal, the secretary impresses the seal on gubernatorial papers. In 1992, the annual salary for the secretary of state was $90,000.

The *state controller* is the chief fiscal officer of the state, accounting for and disbursing state money. As the state's accountant and book-keeper, the controller reports on the financial operations of state and local governments, and requires uniform accounting procedures. The controller's office collects some taxes directly and provides audit resources to ensure that others are collected.

This office also administers the state's personnel payroll system and unclaimed property laws, under which it searches for the rightful owners of money and property turned over to the state. The controller chairs the Public Employees' Retirement System (PERS), State Teach-ers' Retirement System (STRS), the Franchise Tax Board, and the State Lands Commission. The controller is a member of more than 60 boards, commissions, and financing authorities; among them are the Board of Equalization and the Board of Control. In 1992, the annual salary for the controller was $90,000.

The *state treasurer* is banker for the state, paying out state funds when authorized by the controller. The treasurer is also custodian of securities and other valuables deposited with the treasury, seller of state bonds, and investment officer for most state funds. The treasurer's office examines the financial soundness of major debt proposals of certain special districts. The treasurer chairs the Commission on State Finance and serves on several boards, most of which supervise the marketing of bonds. In 1992, the annual salary for the treasurer was $90,000.

The *attorney general* is the chief law enforcement officer of the state, with the obligation to see that laws are uniformly and adequately enforced. As legal adviser, the attorney general interprets laws and renders opinions for the governor, the legislature, state agencies, and some local officials. The attorney general is director of the Depart-ment of Justice which represents the state and its officers in civil litigation and in appeals from superior courts in criminal cases; enforces the state narcotics laws; maintains central fingerprint and other files; administers the state's program of training for local law enforcement officers; and assists peace officers in both criminal and civil investigations.

The attorney general has supervision over all district attorneys and sheriffs and may act in the place of any district attorney if necessary. The attorney general has power to convene a county grand jury to bring matters to its attention. The attorney general's office prepares titles for state initiative and referendum petitions, and titles and digests for all state ballot measures.

With a staff of more than 600 lawyers, the attorney general maintains offices in Sacramento, San Francisco, San Diego, and Los Angeles. In

1992, the annual salary for the attorney general was $102,000.

The *insurance commissioner* became an elected position in 1988. The commissioner is responsible for protecting California's insurance consumers. The commissioner regulates the state's $63 billion-a-year insurance industry, and manages the 835-person Department of Insurance. A special fund agency, the department is supported by insurance fees and receives no taxpayer money. The commissioner enforces the laws of the California Insurance Code and adopts regulations to implement the laws. The department provides information to consumers on insurance rates, complaints against companies and enforcement actions taken against individuals and companies. In 1992, the annual salary for the insurance commissioner was $95,052.

The *Board of Equalization,* one of California's major state revenue agencies, consists of four members elected from equalization districts representing areas of the state nearly equal in population, and the state controller, who serves ex-officio. The board ensures that property throughout the state is assessed uniformly, by guiding and assisting county assessors and prescribing regulations. The board itself assesses the property of railroads and public utilities; administers the retail sales and use taxes; the cigarette, motor fuel, and alcoholic beverage taxes; state taxes on insurance companies; the timber yield tax; the electrical energy surcharge; and the emergency telephone users surcharge. The board is the appellate body for Franchise Tax Board decisions on income and corporate taxes and on property tax relief for senior citizens. In 1992, the annual salary for a member of the Board of Equalization was $95,052.

The *superintendent of public instruction* is elected statewide on a nonpartisan basis. The superintendent directs the Department of Education, executing policies set by the state Board of Education appointed by the governor. In 1992, the annual salary for the superintendent of public instruction was $95,052.

ORGANIZATION OF THE EXECUTIVE BRANCH

THE GOVERNOR'S ADMINISTRATIVE STAFF

The operation of the governor's office varies with each governor, who decides how he or she wishes to manage liaison with departments, the legislature, and the public. In 1992, there were 86 positions in the governor's office, ranging from senior staff to clerical assistance. These staff members are organized into units that assist with particular aspects of executive responsibility.

A major assistant to the governor is the Chief of Staff, who directs and supervises all units in the governor's office, serves as chief aide, and member of the cabinet. Other important assistants include the administrative officer, press secretary, cabinet secretary, legislative secretary, appointments secretary (responsible for maintaining data on upcoming vacancies and potential appointees), and writing and research director.

THE CABINET

As the governor's principal advisory and operational council, the cabinet gives the chief executive a comprehensive view of state operations and aids in policy making and long-range planning. The governor determines the composition of the cabinet, and its members serve at his or her pleasure, playing a major or minor role in policy making as the chief executive wishes. As of January 1992, members of the cabinet were the agency secretaries of Child Development and Education, Environmental Protection; directors of the Departments of Finance, Food and Agriculture, and Industrial Relations; and the governor's chief of staff. Elected officials, various staff members, and other officials may attend cabinet meetings when matters relating to their areas of responsibility are discussed.

AGENCIES AND DEPARTMENTS

To assist the governor in supervising the voluminous activities of state government and maintaining consistency in executive policies, most departments are grouped within "agencies." The secretaries of the agencies provide leadership and policy guidance to the departments in their jurisdictions, serve as communication links between the governor and the departments, and review department budgets and legislative and administrative programs.

In 1992, there were seven agencies: business, transportation, and housing; child development and education; health and welfare; resources; environmental protection; state and consumer services; and, youth and adult corrections. **Figure 6.1** displays the organization of the executive branch. Each department director supervises operations of the divisions in his department and is responsible for their fiscal, administrative, and program performance. The chart does not show the complexity of many of the individual departments, which may include a dozen or more divisions or units. The director reports to the appropriate agency secretary, if any, who is responsible for coordination of related programs, for resolution of problems that go beyond the authority of the department heads, and for overall policy implementation. All communications to the cabinet go through the agency secretary, though frequently the secretary requests a department head attend a cabinet meeting to present information or a position paper. The governor also sometimes holds briefing meetings with department heads.

ADMINISTRATIVE OFFICES

The following offices and departments report directly to the governor:

The *Office of Administrative Law* protects the public from over-

CALIFORNIA STATE GOVERNMENT

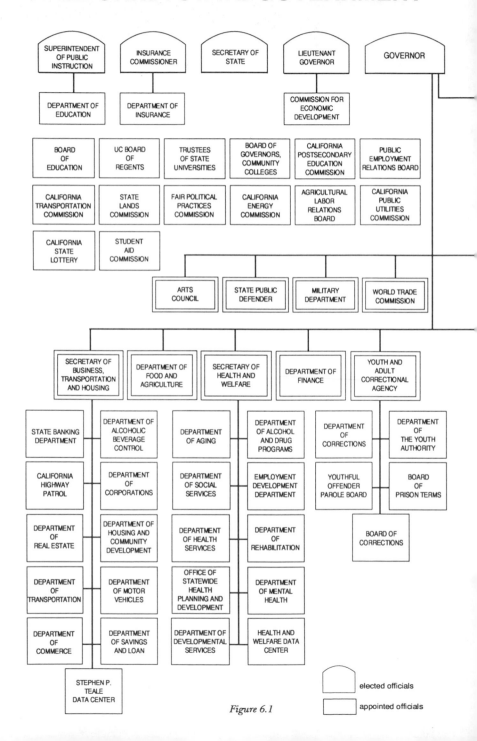

Figure 6.1

THE EXECUTIVE BRANCH

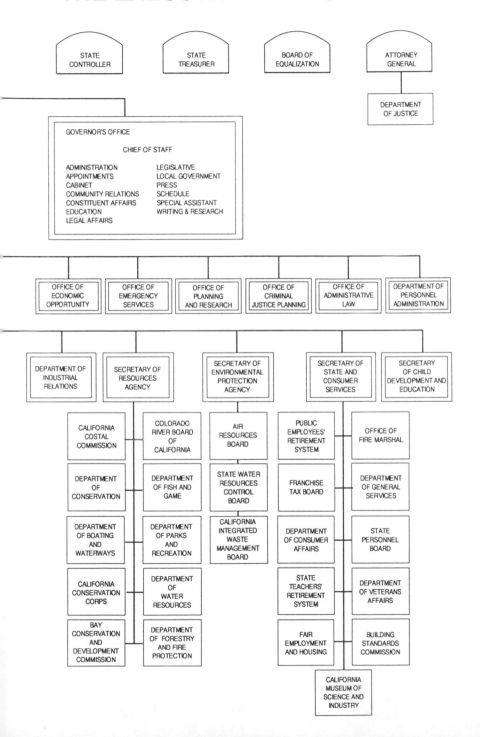

STATE CONTROLLER

STATE TREASURER

BOARD OF EQUALIZATION

ATTORNEY GENERAL

DEPARTMENT OF JUSTICE

GOVERNOR'S OFFICE

CHIEF OF STAFF

ADMINISTRATION
APPOINTMENTS
CABINET
COMMUNITY RELATIONS
CONSTITUENT AFFAIRS
EDUCATION
LEGAL AFFAIRS

LEGISLATIVE
LOCAL GOVERNMENT
PRESS
SCHEDULE
SPECIAL ASSISTANT
WRITING & RESEARCH

OFFICE OF ECONOMIC OPPORTUNITY

OFFICE OF EMERGENCY SERVICES

OFFICE OF PLANNING AND RESEARCH

OFFICE OF CRIMINAL JUSTICE PLANNING

OFFICE OF ADMINISTRATIVE LAW

DEPARTMENT OF PERSONNEL ADMINISTRATION

DEPARTMENT OF INDUSTRIAL RELATIONS

SECRETARY OF RESOURCES AGENCY

SECRETARY OF ENVIRONMENTAL PROTECTION AGENCY

SECRETARY OF STATE AND CONSUMER SERVICES

SECRETARY OF CHILD DEVELOPMENT AND EDUCATION

CALIFORNIA COSTAL COMMISSION

COLORADO RIVER BOARD OF CALIFORNIA

AIR RESOURCES BOARD

PUBLIC EMPLOYEES' RETIREMENT SYSTEM

OFFICE OF FIRE MARSHAL

DEPARTMENT OF CONSERVATION

DEPARTMENT OF FISH AND GAME

STATE WATER RESOURCES CONTROL BOARD

FRANCHISE TAX BOARD

DEPARTMENT OF GENERAL SERVICES

DEPARTMENT OF BOATING AND WATERWAYS

DEPARTMENT OF PARKS AND RECREATION

CALIFORNIA INTEGRATED WASTE MANAGEMENT BOARD

DEPARTMENT OF CONSUMER AFFAIRS

STATE PERSONNEL BOARD

CALIFORNIA CONSERVATION CORPS

DEPARTMENT OF WATER RESOURCES

STATE TEACHERS' RETIREMENT SYSTEM

DEPARTMENT OF VETERANS AFFAIRS

BAY CONSERVATION AND DEVELOPMENT COMMISSION

DEPARTMENT OF FORESTRY AND FIRE PROTECTION

FAIR EMPLOYMENT AND HOUSING

BUILDING STANDARDS COMMISSION

CALIFORNIA MUSEUM OF SCIENCE AND INDUSTRY

regulation and illegal enforcement of unauthorized regulations by reviewing actions on rules proposed by state agencies. More than 130 agencies make regulations which implement or interpret statutes enacted by the legislature. OAL disapproves any regulation that does not meet specific criteria as stated in the Administrative Procedure Act. These criteria specify, among other points, that regulations must be necessary, understandable, and consistent with other laws. OAL encourages and assists individuals who wish to participate in the state's process for ensuring that agency regulations do not create unnecessary red tape.

The *Office of Criminal Justice Planning* implements the governor's public safety plan for California. The office awards federal and state grants to state and local agencies for programs relating to criminal justice and crime prevention and control. OCJP supports criminal justice agencies, local victim/witness organizations, school and community crime prevention programs, and training programs for prosecutors and public defenders. It conducts research, crime analysis, and program evaluation, and develops publications on crime prevention and victim services.

The *Department of Economic Opportunity* administers programs to assist low-income residents in becoming self-sufficient. The department now supervises several federally funded programs, including community services block grants, low-income home energy assistance, and weatherization projects. Services are provided directly and through a network of about 200 community agencies.

The *Office of Emergency Services* maintains a 24-hour disaster warning system and a statewide emergency plan, and helps local jurisdictions develop compatible plans. In addition, the agency distributes federal and state disaster aid funds. OES coordinates mutual aid agreements among state and local fire, rescue, and law enforcement agencies, and maintains a state nuclear power plant emergency response plan. The office has developed a program which uses the state's 24-hour warning system to alert appropriate agencies in emergencies involving toxic or hazardous substances.

The *Department of Personnel Administration* manages the non-merit aspects of the state's personnel system. While the state Personnel Board administers the state's merit program, the DPA represents the governor as the "employer" in all matters concerning state employer/ employee relations. The DPA, in conjunction with departments, reviews existing terms and conditions of civil service employment subject to negotiation, develops management's negotiating positions, represents management in discussions with the 20 employee bargaining units in state government, and administers negotiated memoranda of understanding.

DPA is responsible for administration of the state's job classification plan and for development of personnel management programs and policies pertaining to pay and benefits. The department also provides centralized employee training programs.

The *Office of Planning and Research* serves as the comprehensive state planning policy agency, as planning and research staff to the governor and cabinet, and as a primary liaison with local governments and education. In addition, OPR has statutory responsibilities relating to permit assistance and to environmental and federal project review procedures. The office also administers the California energy extension service, which provides staff outreach and public information programs.

The *Military Department* also reports directly to the office of the governor. It is composed of the offices of the adjutant general, the California Army and Air National Guard (the state militia), the state military reserve, and the naval militia. The department assists state and local authorities in protecting lives and property during natural disasters or civil or other emergencies, and provides military units for federal mobilization in time of national emergency.

The military department also provides training and job counseling at four centers for unemployed youth in Los Angeles, Modesto, Oakland, and Sacramento, to prepare them for job placement with enlistment in the national guard as an option. In cooperation with the state Department of Education and with local school boards, the department administers the *California Cadet Corps*, which trains young people in citizenship and leadership programs.

7

JUDICIAL BRANCH

The state constitution vests the judicial power of the state in the California Supreme Court, Courts of Appeal, Superior Courts, municipal courts, and justice courts. These courts form an independent branch of state government; nevertheless, they are to some degree influenced by the legislature, whose statutes determine much of the courts' operation, and by the governor, who makes most judicial appointments.

ROLE OF THE JUDICIARY

In the division of powers between branches of state government, the judicial branch operates as a check on legislative and executive powers, making sure that these branches do not make or administer laws contrary to constitutional tenets. The judiciary is responsible for seeing that laws are justly and equitably applied in all matters brought before the courts.

RELATION OF STATE TO FEDERAL COURTS

The California judicial system exists side by side with the federal court system. The two systems converge in the U.S. Supreme Court, the final interpreter of the United States Constitution and of all federal law, whether under a statute, treaty, administrative regulation, or the constitution. A case must have been litigated in a lower federal court or involve an issue of federal constitutional law in order for the U.S. Supreme Court to have jurisdiction to hear it. The Supreme Court also determines whether state constitutions and state laws conform to the federal constitution, and state courts are bound by its decisions. If state cases are transferred to the U.S. Supreme Court, they usually go to the federal level from the state's highest court, but it is possible for a case to go directly from a California Court of Appeal to the U.S. Supreme Court.

The federal judicial structure, like that of California, is a hierarchy of courts. Below the Supreme Court are 13 federal Circuit Courts of Appeals. The federal Circuit Court of Appeal is for specialized federal cases, generally arising under the patent, copyright, or custom laws, or involving disputes over contracts with the federal government. The other 12 circuits are regionally organized, and hear appeals from the federal district courts in their regions. The U.S. Court of Appeals for the Ninth Judicial Circuit, headquartered in San Francisco, hears appeals from federal district courts located in California and several other western states. California is divided into four U.S. District Courts, based in San Francisco and San Jose (northern district), Sacramento and Fresno (eastern district), Los Angeles (central district), and San Diego (southern district).

TRIAL AND APPELLATE COURTS

Basically there are two types of California courts: trial and appellate. Cases are tried in a Superior, municipal, or justice court. In these trial courts the facts are determined and a decision is made on the basis of the findings. The decision may be appealed to a higher (appellate) court to determine whether the proper procedures were used in the original trial, or whether the law was correctly applied or interpreted. In most cases, the Supreme Court and Courts of Appeal hear cases only on appeal. The Superior Court hears appeals from the municipal and justice courts.

The state Supreme Court, Courts of Appeal, and Superior Courts have original jurisdiction in some specialized instances where the usual procedures could result in a miscarriage of justice. When this happens, the courts may issue *extraordinary writs:* mandate, requiring a public official or a public body to take a certain action; prohibition, forbidding adjudicatory action; review, reviewing a decision of a lower tribunal; and habeas corpus, ordering that specific relief be granted to a detained individual.

CRIMINAL AND CIVIL CASES

All courts handle both criminal and civil cases. A criminal case involves violation of a law for which a fine or other penalty is prescribed. The offense may be a crime of grave consequence, or a simple traffic violation. Crimes are classified as *felonies* if they are punishable by death or a state prison term. Other offenses are *misdemeanors*, except for minor traffic offenses which are *infractions*. In a criminal case the county district attorney or city attorney represents the people, charges the defendant with an offense, and has the burden of proving the charges if a trial follows. In the courts of appeal and the supreme court, the attorney general represents the state's side of the case. The accused is represented by a private attorney, public defender, or court-appointed attorney. The accused may be allowed to represent himself or herself as counsel. In a criminal case, a jury must agree unanimously on any verdict, whether guilty or not guilty. If the jury cannot agree unanimously one way or the other, it is a "hung jury," and the judge must declare a mistrial.

Civil cases are brought to obtain a court ruling on non-criminal matters. Frequently they are brought to recover damages for injury to persons or property, or to settle disputes over terms of a contract or over property rights. A plaintiff may sue to prevent an act (e.g., the cutting of certain timber) or to compel action (e.g., better street lighting in a specified neighborhood). If a civil trial is by jury, a verdict is reached by agreement of three-fourths of the jurors. Civil proceedings also include matters which come before the court such as a probate of uncontested wills, the dissolution of marriages, adoptions, or the appointment of guardians.

CALIFORNIA COURT SYSTEM

Figure 7.1 shows the structure of California's court system.

JUSTICE AND MUNICIPAL COURTS

Each county is divided by its board of supervisors into judicial districts. In a district of 40,000 or less, there is a justice court with one judge. In a district with a population over 40,000, there is a municipal court. The legislature determines the number of judges in each municipal court district. These range from one to 73. More than 90 percent of the state's judicial business is handled by municipal courts each year.

Since 1989-90, the state and counties have shared the costs of municipal and justice courts, such as salaries and operating expenses, as well as capital outlay for buildings. The county supervisors control the expenditures of justice courts, but the legislature sets the salary of judges and other personnel in municipal courts.

The jurisdiction of justice courts and municipal courts is the same. Both hear civil cases involving up to $25,000 and try all misdemeanors and infractions. Both hold preliminary hearings for felonies, unless the defendant is under 18, in which case a hearing is conducted in the juvenile court. These hearings determine whether there is sufficient evidence to warrant a trial in the Superior Court.

On matters of $5,000 or less, justice and municipal courts may sit as *small claims courts,* where procedures are informal and no attorneys represent the parties. Resort to small claims procedures is entirely voluntary for the plaintiff, even if the plaintiff's claim is for only one dollar. Plaintiffs give up important rights to bring their actions under small claims procedures, including the rights to appeal, to discover evidence possessed by an adversary, and to have the assistance of an attorney. Plaintiffs need not give up these rights, although they do in most cases for less than $1,500, because the lower transaction cost of proceeding in the small claims division is attractive. Only the defendant may appeal from a small claims court decision. Appeals from justice and municipal court decisions go to the superior court.

Judges of justice courts are elected by district for six-year terms. The

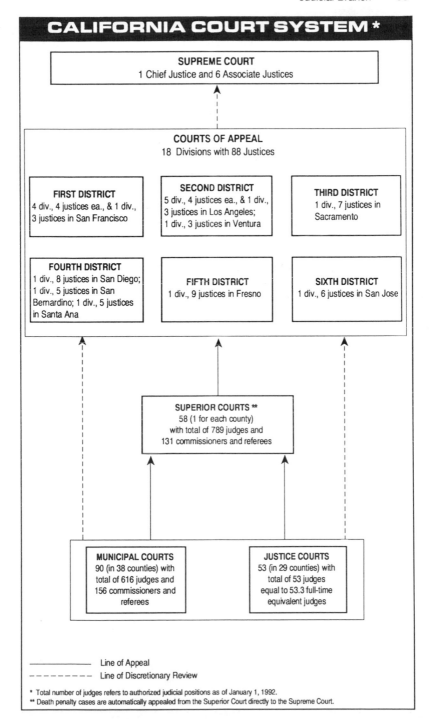

CALIFORNIA COURT SYSTEM *

SUPREME COURT
1 Chief Justice and 6 Associate Justices

COURTS OF APPEAL
18 Divisions with 88 Justices

FIRST DISTRICT
4 div., 4 justices ea., & 1 div.,
3 justices in San Francisco

SECOND DISTRICT
5 div., 4 justices ea., & 1 div.,
3 justices in Los Angeles;
1 div., 3 justices in Ventura

THIRD DISTRICT
1 div., 7 justices in
Sacramento

FOURTH DISTRICT
1 div., 8 justices in San Diego;
1 div., 5 justices in San
Bernardino; 1 div., 5 justices
in Santa Ana

FIFTH DISTRICT
1 div., 9 justices in Fresno

SIXTH DISTRICT
1 div., 6 justices in San Jose

SUPERIOR COURTS **
58 (1 for each county)
with total of 789 judges and
131 commissioners and referees

MUNICIPAL COURTS
90 (in 38 counties) with
total of 616 judges and
156 commissioners and
referees

JUSTICE COURTS
53 (in 29 counties) with
total of 53 judges
equal to 53.3 full-time
equivalent judges

———————— Line of Appeal
– – – – – – – – Line of Discretionary Review

* Total number of judges refers to authorized judicial positions as of January 1, 1992.
** Death penalty cases are automatically appealed from the Superior Court directly to the Supreme Court.

Figure 7.1

office, like that of all judges, is nonpartisan. Vacancies are filled by the board of supervisors. Municipal court judges are also elected by districts for six-year terms, but vacancies are filled by the governor, and the great majority of municipal court judges reach the bench originally by gubernatorial appointment. All judges must have been admitted to practice law in California, and in the case of municipal court judges, at least five years before assuming office.

Many courts employ traffic referees or commissioners to handle routine traffic matters. These subordinate judicial personnel are experienced attorneys selected for their expertise. Their handling of these matters frees judges to hear more serious cases.

SUPERIOR COURTS

Each county also has a Superior Court. Besides hearing appeals from municipal and justice courts, the Superior Court conducts trials in all cases beyond the jurisdiction of the lower courts. Superior Courts hear all felony cases, handle wills and estates, domestic relations, mental competency findings, rights disputes of children and adults, real property titles, writs of mandate, and numerous other civil cases. In large counties some Superior Court judges specialize in certain kinds of cases, such as probate.

At least one judge in each Superior Court sits as judge of the *juvenile court*, which hears cases concerning persons under 18 years of age. Regardless of the alleged offense, juvenile court proceedings are civil, not criminal, in nature. Both the proceedings and procedural safeguards for the the juvenile differ somewhat from those which pertain to an accused adult. Instead of jury trials, for example, there are hearings before the juvenile judge. Routine cases are sometimes heard by court-appointed referees. Since 1982, a "fitness" hearing has been required before a youth over 16 but under 18 accused of a serious crime is treated as a juvenile instead of an adult.

The state constitution requires that an appeal from a Superior Court go directly to the California Supreme Court when the death penalty is involved. Other appeals from Superior Courts go to the court of appeal for each area. Either party may appeal a Superior Court decision.

A Superior Court judge must have been a member of the state bar (admitted to practice law in California) for the ten years preceding entrance into office. The judge is elected by county voters for a six-year term. The governor fills vacancies, and a high proportion of judges come to the bench originally by gubernatorial appointment.

As with municipal courts, the legislature determines the number and salaries of judges. The state and counties share the costs of Superior Courts, including judges' salaries. The state pays costs of homicide trials which exceed an amount equal to five cents per $100 assessed property valuation in the county. Legislation enacted in 1990 provides state funding for 50 percent of Superior Court costs. Counties participating in this program turn over their court fees and fines to the state.

Many Superior Courts appoint commissioners or referees to handle subordinate judicial duties. They are selected for their knowledge and expertise and are generally assigned to hear routine and uncontested cases in the areas of domestic relations, probate, or juvenile law.

COURTS OF APPEAL

California has six appellate districts, each with at least one division. They are headquartered in Fresno, Los Angeles, Sacramento, San Diego, San Francisco, and San Jose. Courts of Appeal sit as three-judge panels with adjudicate cases appealed from the lower courts. Judges study the transcripts of testimony and documents from the original hearing, and attorneys present written briefs and oral arguments. The judges confer in private before voting. Two judges must concur in a decision. All decisions must be in writing. About 12 percent are selected for publication as precedents which lawyers may cite. The Supreme Court has discretion to order an opinion "de-published," which precludes its citation as a precedent. Appeals from their decisions go to the Supreme Court, if that court agrees to hear them. Most cases, however, go no higher than the Courts of Appeal.

The same provisions govern the qualifications and selection of justices for the courts of appeal and the Supreme Court. The state assumes all costs of both courts.

THE CALIFORNIA SUPREME COURT

An appeal is normally heard and decided by the appropriate court of appeal before the Supreme Court considers it. A party dissatisfied with the decision of the Court of Appeal may ask for review by the Supreme Court of any issues that he or she thinks were wrongly decided by the Court of Appeal. Most such petitions for review are denied; the Supreme Court accepts cases to decide important legal questions or to maintain uniformity in the law. Nonetheless, deciding which cases to review occupies a sizable portion of the justices' time. Since 1984 the court has been permitted to focus its review of an appeal on specified issues. Under previous practice the Supreme Court had only the "all or nothing" choice of taking over the whole case after a decision by the Court of Appeal, or letting the Court of Appeal's decision stand in its entirety.

State law provides for the automatic appeal to the state Supreme Court of a judgment sentencing a defendant to death. In such cases the defendant cannot waive the right to appeal.

The Supreme Court has original jurisdiction proceedings for extraordinary relief in the nature of mandate, prohibition, and review. The court also has original jurisdiction in habeas corpus proceedings. The Supreme Court's control over its jurisdiction and that of the courts of appeal includes the power to transfer to itself a case pending before a Court of Appeal, to transfer a case (other than a death penalty appeal) from itself to one of the Courts of Appeal, and to transfer cases among divisions of a Court of Appeal.

In addition, the Supreme Court reviews the recommendations of the Commission on Judicial Performance and the State Bar of California concerning the removal and suspension of judges and attorneys for misconduct.

The state Supreme Court has the final word on the content and application of the law of California. The United States Supreme Court may review a decision of the California Supreme Court only insofar as it turns on an issue of federal law.

The California Supreme Court consists of a chief justice and six associate justices. Four justices must concur in a judgment. Members of the Supreme Court are appointed by the governor and confirmed by the Commission on Judicial Appointments. To be considered for appointment, an individual must be an attorney admitted to practice law in California or have served as a judge of a court of record for ten years immediately preceding appointment.

Terms of office are 12 years, but a justice is frequently appointed to complete the term of his or her predecessor. Constitutional provisions for selection of justices of the Supreme Court and Courts of Appeal are subject to voter approval. Additionally, the Supreme Court reviews the recommendations of the Commission of Judicial Performance and the State Bar of California concerning the discipline of judges and attorneys for misconduct.

The Commission on Judicial Appointments consists of the chief justice, the attorney general, and the senior presiding justice of the affected Court of Appeal. If the incumbent files for re-election, the governor makes no nomination. A candidate runs unopposed, and the ballot question is whether he or she shall be retained in office. For a Supreme Court justice the vote is statewide; for the Court of Appeal, it is by district. If the candidate does not receive a majority affirmation, the governor appoints a different person to the office. Every appointee must receive voter affirmation at the first gubernatorial election following the appointment in order to continue in office.

JUDICIAL COUNCIL

The Judicial Council is the chief administrative agency for the California court system. The chief justice, the chairperson, appoints 14 of its 21 members from among the judges of the Supreme Court, the Courts of Appeal, and the Superior, municipal, and justice courts. Four attorneys are appointed by the state bar, and one member is appointed by each legislative house. Judges and attorneys serve two-year terms. Legislative appointees' terms are determined in each house.

In order to improve the administration of justice, the Judicial Council continually surveys the business of all state courts, including the 18 divisions of the Courts of Appeal, the 58 Superior Courts, and the 143 municipal and justice courts. It makes recommendations to the governor, the legislature, and the various courts. Its powers include the establishment of rules of court procedure, practice, and administration. There are, for example, rules on appeal, on bail, and on photographing, broadcasting, and recording court proceedings.

The state constitution directs the chief justice to expedite the handling of judicial business and to equalize the work of judges. For this reason judges from courts with light workloads may be assigned to those with congested calendars, and, with their consent, retired judges may be assigned to any court.

STATE BAR

The State Bar of California is a public corporation. By constitutional provision every person licensed to practice law in the state is a member, except while serving as a judge of a court other than a justice court. The state Bar's Board of Governors rules on the qualifications for the practice of law. The Committee of Bar Examiners examines candidates and recommends qualified applicants to the state Supreme Court, which grants formal admission to the bar. The State Bar also makes disciplinary recommendations concerning attorneys to the Supreme Court.

DISCIPLINE AND REMOVAL OF JUDGES

Constitutional provisions on the discipline of judges are quite specific. A judge is disqualified from acting as a judge, without loss of salary, while charged with a felony or while the supreme court is considering a recommendation by the Commission on Judicial Performance for the judge's removal or retirement. A judge must be removed if convicted of a felony or crime involving moral turpitude. (During appeal he or she may be suspended without pay.) The Supreme Court makes the decision regarding disciplinary action in other situations, but it may act only on recommendation from the commission.

The Commission on Judicial Performance consists of five judges appointed by the Supreme Court, two attorneys appointed by the state bar, and two non-attorneys appointed by the governor. The commission investigates and may hold hearings on charges against any California judge. It may admonish a judge privately if the judge's conduct does not warrant formal proceedings. On commission recommendation the Supreme Court may retire a judge because of serious disability, or may censure or remove a judge for failure to perform duties, habitual intemperate use of drugs or intoxicants, misconduct in office, or conduct that "brings the judicial office into disrepute." A judge removed by the court is ineligible for subsequent judicial office and, pending further order of the Supreme Court, is suspended from practicing law in the state.

All judges are subject to recall and impeachment. There is no mandatory retirement age, but the state's contributory pension plan for judges offers some inducement to retire at 70.

JURIES

Under our democratic form of government, the citizen also plays an important part in the judicial system, in the role of juror. In many legal cases a jury—panel of ordinary citizens—is entrusted with the task of judging the guilt or innocence of an accused party. While the judge gives direction to the jury and passes final sentence, if any, the jury evaluates the facts, the evidence, and the credibility of witnesses and pronounces the verdict in accordance with the rules given by the trial judge.

A *trial jury* (petit jury) consists of 12 persons, although the legislature may provide for eight-person juries in civil cases in lower courts. A jury trial may be waived in either a civil or criminal case if both parties agree. In that event, the judge makes the decision. Jurors are randomly selected from lists, including those of registered voters, licensed drivers, public utility users and many other sources. There is considerable variety in how the yearly lists are compiled. Most districts employ a jury commissioner for the task. A juror must be a U.S. citizen, 18 years of age, must meet residency requirements of electors, must have adequate health, ordinary intelligence, and understand English. A person may be excused from jury duty if it causes undue hardship to that person or to the public he or she serves.

A *grand jury* of 19 citizens (23 in Los Angeles County) must be summoned in each county every year. The Superior Court judges of the county nominate these jurors, and from their nominations jurors are selected by lot. Grand juries are mainly concerned with matters of county government, such as the condition of jails, the activities of public officials, the records and accounts of agencies, and the efficiency of governmental operations. They may recommend creating new county offices or abolishing existing ones. They handle citizen complaints on matters concerning county government. However, grand juries are becomingly increasingly involved in criminal proceedings. They are not limited in their choice of subjects or depth of inquiry except by their one-year terms of office. The jury submits a final report to the board of supervisors.

When there is reason to believe a crime may have been committed, at the request of the district attorney the grand jury may hear witnesses and determine if the evidence is sufficient to warrant a trial. If so, it returns to the court an indictment of the accused. However, most persons are now brought to trial through preliminary hearings in municipal and justice courts.

Some counties have two grand juries, one to function as governmental watchdog and the other to return criminal indictments.

A *jury of inquest* (coroner's jury) of six to 15 persons may be summoned by the coroner to hear testimony in cases of death in unusual circumstances, or when violence, suicide, or criminal activity is suspected. The jury's role is to determine whether further action is necessary.

LEGAL SERVICES

In California, several federal and state agencies provide legal assistance for people who cannot afford lawyers.

In criminal cases, an indigent defendant may be represented by either a public defender or a private lawyer appointed directly by the court. Income, size of family, and debts are among the factors determining eligibility for free or reduced-cost counsel. More than half the people accused of serious crimes in California use public defenders or court-appointed counsel.

County public defenders represent their clients in the trial courts. Any county or group of counties may establish a public defender's office. Many counties in the state either have such an office or contract with the state to handle cases for the indigent. Other counties provide defense in ways varying from court appointment on a case-by-case basis to annual contracts with the county bar association.

The office of *state public defender* provides legal representation for indigents before the supreme court and the courts of appeal. The state public defender is appointed by the governor to a minimum term of four years The office is authorized to contract with county public defenders, private attorneys and others to provide legal services.

Responsibility for legal aid in civil cases has been assumed principally by the federal government. The Legal Services Corporation provides federal funds for neighborhood legal offices, which offer assistance in civil actions such as divorces, property damage, personal injuries, contracts, and bankruptcies. California Rural Legal Assistance and California Indian Legal Services are other corporation programs. Federal funds also support the Western Center on Law and Poverty which recruits and trains poverty-law attorneys, and files class action lawsuits on special legal problems of the poor.

RUNNING THE GOVERNMENT

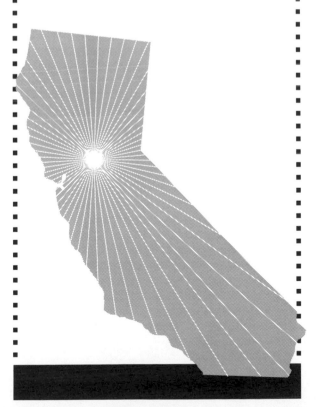

8

BUSINESS, TRANSPORTATION, AND HOUSING AGENCY

The Business, Transportation, and Housing Agency in the executive branch encompasses three groupings of departments and boards. In one cluster are business-related and regulatory departments; in another, transportation-related departments and, in the third, housing-related agencies.

BUSINESS, TRANSPORTATION, AND HOUSING AGENCY

Department of Real Estate	Department of Transportation
State Banking Department	Department of Motor Vehicles
Department of Corporations	Department of the California
Department of Savings and	Highway Patrol
Loan	Office of Traffic Safety
Department of Alcoholic	Department of Housing and
Beverage Control	Community Development
Department of Commerce	California Housing Finance
Stephen P. Teale Data Center	Agency

Figure 8.1

BUSINESS-RELATED DEPARTMENTS

State as well as federal laws protect the public interest by establishing and maintaining standards for business and financial practices. The following state departments administer laws and regulations which safeguard the solvency of financial institutions and protect the public from unscrupulous practices.

DEPARTMENT OF REAL ESTATE

The Department of Real Estate prepares and distributes public reports on offerings of subdivided property which fall under its jurisdiction. It tests all license applicants to guarantee that those who conduct real estate transactions as agents or brokers are competent and qualified. To prevent fraud, deceit, and misrepresentation in the real estate marketplace, the department investigates consumer complaints and educates the public and professional communities regarding laws and regulations governing real estate transactions.

STATE BANKING DEPARTMENT

The State Banking Department administers laws, regulations, and licensing for state-chartered banks, foreign banking corporations, money transmitters, payment instruments, money order and trust companies. It is responsible for assuring that public funds deposited by local agencies in banks and savings and loans are secured, as required by law. It examines its licensees to ensure that they operate in a safe and sound manner.

DEPARTMENT OF CORPORATIONS

The Department of Corporations establishes and enforces regulations on the sale of securities and franchises to protect the public from improper practices. It supervises financial institutions, excluding banks and savings and loan associations, which lend or receive funds. These include escrow companies, credit unions, industrial loan companies, and personal property brokers. The department also supervises health care service plans.

DEPARTMENT OF SAVINGS AND LOAN

The Department of Savings and Loan licenses, supervises, and regulates state-chartered savings and loan associations. Deposit insurance is provided to both state-chartered and federally-chartered savings and loan associations by the Federal Deposit Insurance Corporation.

DEPARTMENT OF ALCOHOLIC BEVERAGE CONTROL

The Department of Alcoholic Beverage Control issues licenses and administers laws governing the manufacture, importation, distribution, and sale of alcoholic beverages. ABC may deny, suspend, or revoke licenses for good cause. Department decisions may be appealed to the three-member Alcoholic Control Appeals Board, which is appointed by the governor with Senate confirmation.

DEPARTMENT OF COMMERCE

The Department of Commerce promotes business development and the creation of jobs in the state. It coordinates federal, state, and local economic development policies and allocates federal development funds. This department provides information and statistics on California's economy, products, tourism, and international trade. It also assists in small business development and in plant location and capital investment for new or expanding businesses.

STEPHEN P. TEALE DATA CENTER

The Stephen P. Teale Data Center is the largest and most comprehensive computing facility within California state government. It provides automated data processing services to more than 200 state governmental agencies via a sophisticated statewide communications network. It was established by the legislature to provide centralized computing capability to state agencies.

TRANSPORTATION-RELATED DEPARTMENTS

Programs that concern transportation and the safe use of the highways are carried out by the Department of Transportation, the Department of Motor Vehicles, the Department of the California Highway Patrol, and the Office of Traffic Safety.

DEPARTMENT OF TRANSPORTATION

The Department of Transportation plans, coordinates, and implements the state's transportation systems in conjunction with regional agencies, local governments, and the private sector. Caltrans has 16 divisions, among which are four with broad planning responsibilities:

The *Division of Transportation Planning* is responsible for the department's highway system planning consisting of route concept reports and route development plans for each state route and a system management plan for each of the department's 12 districts. This division also assists regional transportation planning agencies to develop long-range plans and resolve regional transportation problems.

The *Division of Mass Transportation* prepares feasibility studies and develops policies to expand the use of public transportation services. This division supports local transit programs by reviewing plans, providing consultation services, and helping obtain grants and other financial aid.

The *Division of Highways Program Development* participates in the development of the State Transportation Improvement Program or STIP, which is adopted by the California Transportation Commission. This division also maintains a technical information base on the state highway system.

The *Division of Aeronautics* is responsible for development of the California airport system plan. It also administers financial aid programs for public use airports, enforces standards for airport safety, administers airport noise regulations, and issues operating permits for airports and heliports.

Other divisions of the Department of Transportation are responsible for the maintenance of more than 15,200 miles of state highways, the purchase of right of way, the design and construction of additions to the highway system, operation of the nine state toll bridges, administration of federal aid, local assistance, and ridesharing services.

The *California Transportation Commission,* though independent of the Business, Transportation, and Housing Agency, works closely with the Department of Transportation. It has broad responsibilities for the planning and funding of almost every mode of transportation. Every two years it adopts a seven-year State Transportation Improvement Program for capital expenditures by the Department of Transportation. In developing this plan the commission considers a broad range of data and public input.

The commission submits to the legislature an annual report summarizing policies, decisions, major allocations, and important transportation issues. The commission's nine members are appointed by the governor to serve four-year terms.

DEPARTMENT OF MOTOR VEHICLES

The Department of Motor Vehicles protects the public interest and promotes public safety on the state's roads and highways through these principal programs:

The *Vehicle and Vessel Registration and Titling* program identifies vehicle ownership through registration and titling.

The *Driver Licensing and Control* program licenses drivers, promotes safe driving practices, and exercises control over drivers with mental or physical impairments or those who have been judged to be unsafe.

The *Occupational Licensing and Regulation* program administers regulations pertaining to persons and companies engaged in the manufacture, transportation, sale, distribution, and dismantling of vehicles. It also regulates driving schools and traffic violator schools.

The *Financial Responsibility* program enforces the carrying of motor vehicle insurance by suspending the driving privilege of uninsured vehicle drivers and/or owners.

The department's services also include the issuance of photo identification cards to persons of any age and license plates and placards to disabled persons, who thereby gain access to parking spots for the handicapped or exemption from parking meter fees.

DEPARTMENT OF THE CALIFORNIA HIGHWAY PATROL

The Department of the California Highway Patrol is responsible for ensuring the safe, lawful, and efficient use of the state roadway system. This criminal justice agency protects life and property through accident control, congestion relief, law enforcement, and transportation services. The department administers three programs for motorists:

The *Traffic Management* program encompasses patrol of highways and enforcement of the California Vehicle Code, aid for motorists, investigation of accidents, and help for other law enforcement agencies as necessary. Traffic officers not only patrol the state freeway system and roads in unincorporated areas, but also have authority to act on roads in incorporated areas.

The *Regulation and Inspection* program involves inspection of school buses and commercial vehicles and terminals to ensure that trucks are in safe mechanical condition and comply with California vehicle weight laws. It regulates the loading and transportation of specific materials, including hazardous commodities.

The *Vehicle Ownership Security* program includes recovery of stolen vehicles and identification and renumbering of vehicles when identification plates have been removed or are missing.

OFFICE OF TRAFFIC SAFETY

The Office of Traffic Safety evaluates and approves state and local highway safety projects supported by federal funds. This office is also responsible for updating the state's highway safety plan, providing technical assistance to state and local agencies in planning traffic safety, and coordinating ongoing traffic safety programs.

HOUSING-RELATED AGENCIES

State programs that concern housing are carried out by the Department of Housing and Community Development and the California Housing Finance Agency. Regulations against housing discrimination are enforced by the Department of Fair Employment and Housing in the State and Consumer Services Agency.

DEPARTMENT OF HOUSING AND COMMUNITY DEVELOPMENT

The Department of Housing and Community Development assists local government, community organizations, and private business in providing housing throughout the state.

The *Division of Codes and Standards* develops housing and building standards, enforces health and safety codes, and is responsible for registration and titling of mobile and floating homes in the state.

The *Division of Community Affairs* is responsible for administering 30 programs which provide grants, deferred loans, and conventional loans. It also offers technical assistance for the development of affordable housing.

The *Division of Housing Policy Development* identifies housing and community development needs, develops recommendations to meet those needs, and researches specific issues relating to the provision of housing and suitable living environments.

CALIFORNIA HOUSING FINANCE AGENCY

The California Housing Finance Agency has financing powers to provide housing for individuals and families of low and moderate income. It issues tax-exempt revenue bonds to make or ensure below-market interest rate loans to meet housing needs. Loans for housing ownership are made indirectly through private lending institutions; loans for rental housing are made directly to qualified borrowers or indirectly through private lending institutions.

The California Housing Finance Agency has an 11-member board of directors, appointed by the governor to six-year terms.

9

HEALTH AND WELFARE AGENCY

State government, in cooperation with federal and local government, plays an important role in protecting the physical, mental, economic, and social well-being of the residents of California. The Health and Welfare Agency administers state and federal programs for health care, social services, public assistance, job training, and rehabilitation, with approximately 50 percent of its budget coming from federal funds. Responsibility for administering the major programs providing direct services is divided among a number of departments and offices grouped under the Health and Welfare Agency.

HEALTH AND WELFARE AGENCY

Department of Social Services
Department of Aging
Employment Development
  Department
Department of Health Services
Department of Mental Health
Department of Developmental
  Services
Department of Rehabilitation

Department of Alcohol and
  Drug Programs
Office of Statewide Health
  Planning and Development
Emergency Medical Services
  Authority
Health and Welfare Data
  Center

Figure 9.1

DEPARTMENT OF SOCIAL SERVICES

The Department of Social Services manages California's income maintenance and social service programs, some of which are funded by the state, some by the federal government.

The *Welfare Program* division has overall responsibility for programs which provide financial assistance to needy individuals. The division also supervises job training, and employment programs and other services. Division programs include:

The *Aid to Families with Dependent Children* program provides cash grants to those children and their parents and guardians whose income is insufficient to provide for basic needs. Eligibility is limited to families whose children are needy because of the death, incapacity, continued absence, or unemployment of a parent. The federal government contributes 50 percent, the state 47.5 percent, and the county 2.5 percent toward the cost of grants to non-refugee AFDC recipients eligible under the federal family group and unemployed parent programs. In California, AFDC programs are administered by the counties, with state supervision.

The *Food Stamps* program increases the food purchasing power of eligible low-income people by enabling them to use coupons to buy food at authorized grocery stores. Federally funded, it is administered through counties under state supervision.

The *Child Support Enforcement* program operates in cooperation with district attorneys and county welfare departments to obtain child support payments from absent welfare and non-welfare parents.

The *Greater Avenues for Independence* program is designed to increase the employment of recipients of Aid to Families with Dependent Children. Enacted by the legislature in 1985, this program requires welfare recipients whose children are three years of age or older to look for work. GAIN is administered through counties, which provide skills assessment and supply available job search, transportation, and child care. The county and the client develop a contract outlining the duties and responsibilities of each and the services to be supplied by the county. Recipients who remain unemployed after fulfilling the terms of the contract and those who do not complete the training or education agreed upon are assigned to work for a public or nonprofit agency.

The *Refugee and Immigration Programs Branch* administers the federally-funded Refugee Resettlement Program which provides cash, medical assistance, and social services to aid refugees. Social services are usually provided by private nonprofit agencies contracting with DSS for programs such as employment assistance, vocational training and English as a second language. Since 1983, the RIPB has been responsible for administering refugee employment and training programs through county agencies.

The RIPB also administers the federally-funded State Legalization Impact Assistance Grant, which pays for education and other services which are needed to allow undocumented aliens to qualify for legal resident status under the Immigration Control and Reform Act.

In 1990-91, approximately 320,000 refugees in California received cash assistance through programs administered by the Department of Social Services.

The **Adult and Family Services** division supervises and monitors county administration of social service programs mandated by the state, such as information and referral, protective services for children and adults, and in-home supportive services. It administers the state's adoption and foster care placement and rate settling programs, as well as the Supplemental Security Income/State Supplementary Payment program.

SSI/SSP provides cash grants to eligible aged, visually impaired, and disabled individuals. The federal government through Social Security offices determines eligibility and issues the payments. The federal government funds the SSI grant; the state funds the SSP grant.

Other special aid programs provide grants for emergencies, and food allowances for guide dogs.

The *Community Care Licensing* **division** is responsible for licensing and monitoring approximately 60,000 community care non-medical facilities serving approximately 580,000 persons. Facility categories include family day care, child care centers, adult day care centers, foster family homes, small family homes, group homes, adult residential facilities, rehabilitation facilities, facilities for the elderly, and home finding and adoption agencies.

• DSS has delegated licensing authority for foster family homes to 47 of the 58 counties. Thirty of the 47 counties have chosen to accept licensing authority for family day care as well as foster family homes. The state is responsible for all other categories of licensure within the counties.

• Contracting counties and the district offices perform pre-application facility evaluations, application processing, license issuance, annual review of residential facilities and child care centers, response to complaints, renewal licensing, and related functions to ensure that facilities meet licensing standards before they are licensed and continue to meet those standards after obtaining a license.

• Staff members routinely visit contract counties to ensure compliance with licensing standards. Investigations and audits of community care facilities are conducted to detect or verify suspected violations of client health, safety, and financial, legal, or personal rights. Documented violations may result in administrative or court actions to determine if a facility may continue to operate.

• Regional Child Care Ombudsman program provides information to the general public and parents on child care licensing standards and regulations. The program also serves as a liaison for local business, community, law enforcement, labor, and education groups, as well as child care providers and consumers, to provide information about licensing standards and regulations. It disseminates information on the state's licensing role and activities, child care resource and referral agencies, and other child care programs. It acts as a liaison to child care resource and referral agencies to provide current information on licensing regulations, procedures, violations, revocations, and activities, and investigates and seeks to resolve complaints and concerns communicated on behalf of children served by a child day care facility.

The *Disability Evaluation* **division** determines the medical and vocational eligibility of state residents under the disability insurance, supplemental security income, and medically needy programs of the

Social Security Act.

DEPARTMENT OF AGING

The Department of Aging is the principal unifying organization for federal, state, and local agencies serving more than four million older Californians. As the state's unit on aging, it fulfills goals outlined in the Older Americans Act to create options for seniors. The department works with 33 area agencies on aging throughout the state. Under the department's direction these area agencies manage a wide array of services to seniors in the community including nutrition programs, social services, and health insurance counseling.

The department has assumed leadership in constructing a community-based, long-term care structure, with multi-purpose senior services, adult day health care, and support programs. It advocates development of an environment that respects and values older citizens and improves the quality of life for them.

The *California Commission on Aging* serves as an advisory body to the governor, the legislature, and the Department of Aging and acts as principal advocate for the state's seniors. The commission consists of 25 members appointed to three year terms by the governor, the Senate Rules Committee, and the speaker of the Assembly.

EMPLOYMENT DEVELOPMENT DEPARTMENT

The Employment Development Department provides a job service program that matches job seekers and employers and helps welfare recipients and other disadvantaged people prepare for employment through job training. The department also administers the unemployment insurance (UI) and disability insurance (DI) programs and collects UI, DI, and personal income tax withholding from California employers. Most EDD services are provided with federal funds under agreements and contracts with the U.S. Department of Labor.

Job Service **programs** are offered through more than 200 EDD field offices located throughout the state. In addition to job placement, EDD offices also offer information on current labor market conditions, job and employer requirements, job-seeking methods, and counseling. The department also administers a number of job-training programs, the major one being the federally funded Job Training Partnership Act. This program provides training and assistance to special adult and youth groups, such as summer youth employees, displaced workers, veterans, and older workers.

Service centers operate in nine economically depressed areas throughout the state to assist individuals vocationally handicapped by lack of skills or limited education. The centers coordinate government and community services to help individuals become employable and find jobs.

Job agents working out of EDD field offices assist with job placement for those considered severely disadvantaged because of factors such as racial discrimination, poor education, and a background of poverty.

Insurance and tax collection **programs** administered by the Employment Development Department include the following:

• The unemployment insurance program operates under state law to provide benefit payments to eligible workers who have become unemployed through no fault of their own. UI is financed by contribution from employers who pay a tax based on a percentage of the wages of workers covered by the program. Under this plan the worker receives payments for a limited number of weeks, provided he or she is able and willing to accept a suitable job.

• The disability insurance program operates under state law to provide benefit payments to eligible workers who cannot work due to illness or injury that is not related to their employment. (Workers' compensation covers job-related illness or injury.) Disability insurance is financed entirely by workers through a payroll tax on their earnings. Both wage ceilings and tax rates are set by law. In 1992, the tax rate was 1.25 percent of $31,767 in annual wages, or a maximum tax of $397.09.

• The employment tax programs administered by EDD involve the collection of taxes relating to employment: unemployment insurance, disability insurance, and personal income tax withholding. These taxes, affecting approximately 15 million wage earners, are collected from more than 750,000 California employers. Although the personal income tax is principally the responsibility of the Franchise Tax Board, EDD is responsible for collecting withholding payments.

• The California Unemployment Insurance Appeals Board is an independent agency; however, EDD is required by law to provide it with equipment, supplies, and staff services. The board is composed of seven members, five appointed by the governor and one each by the Senate Rules Committee and the Assembly speaker. The board hears appeals from decisions made by administrative law judges in California's 11 Offices of Appeal. Appeals and petitions cover the areas of unem-ployment insurance, disability insurance, and employment taxes.

DEPARTMENT OF HEALTH SERVICES

The Department of Health Services provides medical assistance to California's low-income residents through the Medi-Cal program and administers a broad range of public health programs, including assistance to local health agencies and the licensing of health care facilities.

Medi-Cal is a joint federal-state program to provide health care services to low-income people. (Medicare is a different federal health insurance program for people 65 and older and some people under 65 who are disabled.) Recipients of AFDC and SSI/SSP, who already receive cash grants, automatically qualify for Medi-Cal. Others may qualify if the amount of income and assets cannot adequately cover both living expenses and medical costs. In these cases, the recipients of health care contribute to the costs depending upon their ability to pay.

Medi-Cal recipients are entitled to a variety of health services, including inpatient and outpatient hospital and laboratory services and nursing home care. The program will not pay for some medical expenses, such as the cost of certain drugs and some surgical procedures.

Prevention Services **programs** support and provide resources and technical assistance to local health departments, community organizations, other DHS components, and state agencies.

These programs are designed to incorporate prevention services and messages in comprehensive primary health care, coordinate the surveillance of communicable diseases, minimize the incidence and prevalence of communicable diseases, and provide a comprehensive risk management effort.

Primary Care and Family Health **programs** assure access to culturally sensitive, comprehensive and coordinated family-centered primary care services through:

California Children Services. Provides specialized medical care and rehabilitation for physically handicapped children whose families are partially or wholly unable to provide for such care.

Child Health and Disability Prevention. Reduces the incidence of preventive physical and mental illness and disability among California's children and youth by providing health screens and assessments.

Genetic Disease. Reduces the burden of disability and death caused from disorders which are inherited or genetically determined.

Maternal and Child Health. Assures that all mothers and children have access to quality maternal and child health services.

Office of Family Planning. Provides family planning services to California citizens of childbearing age and promotes the health of potential parents through educational and preventive clinical services.

Primary Care. Improves the health status of special population groups living in medically underserved areas of California.

Women, Infant, and Children (WIC) Supplemental Food program. Provides services to low-income pregnant, postpartum, and breastfeeding women, infants, and children under five years of age who are at nutritional risk. Services include nutritious supplemental food, nutrition education, and referral.

The *Licensing and Certification* **program** regulates approximately 3,400 public and private health facilities, from acute care hospitals to adult day care centers. On-going evaluation and inspection of facilities for compliance with state and federal standards are carried out regularly. Facilities with deficiencies may be subject to fines or revocation of their licenses.

THE DEPARTMENT OF MENTAL HEALTH

The Department of Mental Health is the state agency responsible for overseeing California's mental health system. Its goal is to enable children and adults with serious emotional disturbances or disabling mental illness to access appropriate services and programs.

The responsibility for the direct provision of these services lies with the counties. However, as the federally designated mental health authority, the State Department of Mental Health must ensure that certain standards are met and priority populations served. This is achieved through performance contracts and enactment of certain regulations. Additionally, the Department oversees the protection of patients' rights.

The *Lanterman-Petris-Short Act of 1969* established the civil commitment process for persons who are gravely disabled or dangerous to themselves or others. The act defines the instances in which a person may be involuntarily detained for psychiatric evaluation and treatment. Communities are required to provide mental health treatment in the least restrictive setting. This requirement, coupled with the long-term trend toward treating mentally disordered persons in or near their own communities, means that the majority of mentally ill persons in California today are treated in community settings rather than in state hospitals.

Approximately 320,000 individuals receive mental health services in California annually. Only 20,000 of these enter state hospitals, with the remainder treated within the community. At any given time approximately 5,000 patients are receiving treatment for mental illness in state hospitals.

State hospitals (see **Figure 9.2**) provide services to mentally disabled and developmentally disabled patients. Four of the 11 state hospitals are operated by the Department of Mental Health and provide services to the mentally disabled. The department also manages programs for the mentally disabled at Camarillo, one of the seven state hospitals serving the developmentally disabled and administered by the Department of Developmental Services. Two state hospitals which primarily serve patients coming via the correctional system, whether it be the courts or the prison system, are Atascadero and Patton State Hospitals.

DEPARTMENT OF DEVELOPMENTAL SERVICES

The Department of Developmental Services administers care, treatment and training throughout California to children and adults with developmental disabilities. Developmental disabilities include mental retardation, cerebral palsy, epilepsy, autism, and similar conditions. The department administers seven state developmental centers (state hospitals) and contracts with 21 regional centers to provide services locally. Major activities of the department include reducing the incidence and severity of developmental disabilities through prevention, increasing available services to previously underserved populations, establishing quality assurance standards, and increasing the self-sufficiency of people with developmental disabilities in the most

STATE HOSPITALS AND DEVELOPMENTAL CENTERS

Administration	Hospital	County Location
Department of Mental Health	Atascadero	San Luis Obispo
	Metropolitan	Los Angeles
	Napa*	Napa
	Patton	San Bernardino
	Developmental Center	
Department of Developmental Services	Agnews	Santa Clara
	Camarillo*	Ventura
	Fairview	Orange
	Lanterman	Los Angeles
	Porterville	Tulare
	Sonoma	Sonoma
	Stockton	San Joaquin

* Also offer programs for mentally disabled under Department of Mental Health management.

Figure 9.2

efficient and cost-effective manner.

The *State Council on Developmental Disabilities* has 17 members appointed by the governor and four ex-officio members. The council prepares an annual state plan for persons with developmental disabilities and monitors and evaluates implementation of this plan. The council is assisted in the planning process by 13 local area boards.

DEPARTMENT OF REHABILITATION

The mission of the Department of Rehabilitation is to provide, purchase and advocate services, and to develop and encourage programs which will enhance the ability of persons with disabilities to obtain or retain suitable employment and live independently.

Services such as training programs, individualized counseling, placement, and follow-up assistance are administered in over 115 offices throughout the state. Medical, psychological and vocational evaluations may be used to determine if someone is eligible for services and to help determine the type and level of services a particular consumer may need.

The Department of Rehabilitation works to prevent and remove architectural and program barriers to persons with disabilities. It also advocates for persons with disabilities by educating and informing the general public and by implementing federal and state requirements for affirmative action and anti-discrimination.

DEPARTMENT OF ALCOHOL AND DRUG PROGRAMS

The Department of Alcohol and Drug Programs exists to lead and coordinate the state's effort to prevent or minimize the problems associated with alcohol and other drugs. The department operates in partnership with the 58 county governments, giving planning and financial assistance to locally operated programs.

The department's primary goal is to eliminate addiction and other problems associated with alcohol and other drug use. To that end, it funds or oversees a network of prevention, treatment and recovery programs for both the general population and special target groups, working within a total budget of approximately $312 million annually.

Major services provided through the state/county partnership include:

• Treatment/recovery services—individual, group, and educational sessions provided in residential or nonresidential detoxification, treatment, and recovery settings.

• Detoxification programs—supporting and assisting individuals during a period of planned withdrawal from alcohol and drug dependency and providing support systems to assure continued recovery.

• Prevention of alcohol and other drug problems, through a comprehensive, community-based strategy.

OFFICE OF STATEWIDE HEALTH PLANNING AND DEVELOPMENT

The Office of Statewide Health Planning and Development is responsible for implementing state health planning policy as it affects the delivery of health services, the supply of health personnel, and the seismic safety of health facilities. It is the single state agency responsible for collection and disclosure of all health facility fiscal and utilization data.

The office administers the state Certificate of Need Law, which requires health facilities to seek state approval of some capital outlay projects. In that respect the office works with 12 local health systems agencies to develop a statewide plan of health resource needs. It also administers the state seismic safety program of health facility construction and the development of certain types of public and nonprofit health facilities through state mortgage insurance.

The office promotes the use of health professionals in non-traditional demonstration projects to expand health care services, and it supports the training of physicians, physician assistants, and nurse practitioners in medically underserved areas.

EMERGENCY MEDICAL SERVICES AUTHORITY

The Emergency Medical Services Authority was legislatively created in 1980 to develop standardized emergency medical services (EMS) systems throughout California. Funding for these programs is provided through the state General Fund and the federal Preventative Medical and Health Services Block Grant Fund.

The *Emergency Medical Services* **section** of the authority is responsible for developing guidelines and regulations for day-to-day emergency medical systems components including manpower and training, communications, transportation, assessment of hospitals and critical care centers, system organization and management, data collection and evaluation, public information and education, and disaster response. These components are implemented by local and regional EMS systems.

The *Disaster Medical Services* **section** of the authority is responsible for planning and, if necessary, managing the state's medical response to a major disaster. This section has developed plans and procedures for mobilizing medical supplies, equipment, and personnel to meet the medical needs of disaster victims.

HEALTH AND WELFARE DATA CENTER

The Health and Welfare Data Center, established in 1978, provides centralized computer service to Health and Welfare Agency Programs. Its primary responsibilities are to ensure that the necessary computer resources are available to meet the needs of the departments and offices in the agency and that effective and economical use of these resources is made in support of program administration.

10

RESOURCES AND ENVIRONMENTAL PROTECTION AGENCIES

California has a long history of government regulation of its resources. Concern over water is as old as the state itself. California's Board of Fish Commissioners, established by 1870 to maintain "fish breederies," was the first wildlife conservation agency in the nation. By 1885 the state had a Board of Forestry.

Since the mid-1960s traditional concern for ecological conservation and use of natural resources has become just one aspect of a broader concern to preserve environmental quality. A growing alertness to the side effects of single-purpose planning and to the direct effect of major public works and policies on environment, land use, and distribution of people has led to much legislation emphasizing environmental goals.

CALIFORNIA ENVIRONMENTAL QUALITY ACT

The California Environmental Quality Act was enacted in 1970 as the state's primary environmental protection law. CEQA requires all state and local agencies to consider the environmental effects of a proposed

RESOURCES AGENCY

Department of Water Resources	State Lands Commission
Department of Forestry and Fire Protection	Energy Resources, Conservation and Development Commission
Department of Parks and Recreation	California Tahoe Conservancy
	Colorado River Board
Department of Fish and Game	California Coastal Commission
Department of Boating and Waterways	California Coastal Conservancy
	San Francisco Bay Conservation
Department of Conservation	and Development Commission
California Conservation Corps	

Figure 10.1

project and to reject it if alternative measures are available and feasible that would significantly reduce the project's impact on California's lands, air, and waters.

Proposals for plans, policies, and development projects are subject to CEQA requirements, except for several categorically exempt activities, such as reconstruction, minor alterations, or emergency projects. The requirements of the act apply whether the project is proposed by a private party (e.g., to build a subdivision) or by a public agency (e.g., to form a special district or build a freeway).

CEQA requires the project proponent to prepare an *environmental assessment* to identify and analyze environmental effects of the proposed project. If at that time the reviewing agency considers the proposal to be environmentally significant, the applicant must prepare an *environmental impact report* (EIR). The EIR must include a description of the existing environment, the environmental impact of the proposal including significant cumulative impacts, and recommended measures to minimize damage to the environment.

If the reviewing agency finds that a project will have no significant adverse impact on the environment, it may issue a *negative declaration*. If, after public review, the negative declaration is adopted, the project is permitted to proceed. CEQA allows approval of a project despite significant adverse impacts if the project has overriding social and economic benefit. In addition, a project may be approved if the proponent agrees to specified mitigating measures that will reduce its detrimental effect on the environment. A project can be rejected if it is environmentally unacceptable.

Citizen involvement plays a vital role in the environmental review process. The public has a right to review and comment on the environmental assessment and the draft EIR. The final EIR must include a written response to each public comment. Once a project has been approved or rejected, a citizen or public interest group can appeal the decision by challenging it through a lawsuit.

RESOURCES AGENCY

The Resources Agency administers policies, laws, and regulations concerned with many natural resources of California. It functions through seven departments, which have boards and commissions associated with them. In addition, seven essentially independent boards, commissions, or conservancies are also assigned to the Resources Agency for administrative purposes.

DEPARTMENT OF WATER RESOURCES

The Department of Water Resources is responsible for protecting and managing California's water resources. It is authorized to develop supplies adequate for all its population from all available sources, including transfer of water to areas of need, desalting, reclaiming, and recycling of waste water. It maintains public safety through flood water conservation management, supervision of dams, and safe drinking water projects.

The *California Water Plan* is a general guide for all water management activities; and studies water supplies by assessing dry year criteria and service area allocations, water exchanges among systems, reuse of waste water, effects of water quality regulations, energy impacts, surface water developments, drainage, and use of surface and ground water supplies. This water plan was adopted in 1959 by the legislature and is periodically updated by DWR.

The *State Water Project* provides water along a 600-mile route from Plumas County in the north to Los Angeles, San Bernardino, Riverside, and San Diego counties in southern California. (See Figure 10.2.) The largest project reservoir is Lake Oroville on the Feather River. Water released from this reservoir flows down the Feather and Sacramento rivers and through the Sacramento-San Joaquin Delta. South of the delta, water is pumped into the 444-mile long California Aqueduct to serve the San Francisco Bay area, the San Joaquin Valley, and southern California.

The initial funding for the State Water Project was provided by the $1.75 billion Water Resources Development Bond Act, approved by the voters in 1960. Bonds issued under this act are being repaid by the 29 public water distributing agencies that have contracted for project water. Other sources of financing are the sale of power and water revenue bonds, federal reimbursement for flood control features and a portion of the state's tideland oil revenues, in addition to General Fund money for recreation and wildlife enhancement.

The *California Water Commission* is a nine-member board which advises the director of the Department of Water Resources. Its members are appointed by the governor to four-year terms. The commission conducts hearings and investigations in all parts of the state and makes recommendations to the director of the Department of Water Resources on matters under the director's jurisdiction. It advises on the annual water project budget and each year advises Congress on proposed appropriations for federally-built water facilities in California.

The *Reclamation Board* in the Department of Water Resources has various specific responsibilities for the construction, maintenance, and protection of flood control levees within the Sacramento and San Joaquin River valleys. Its seven members are appointed by the governor.

DEPARTMENT OF FORESTRY AND FIRE PROTECTION

The Department of Forestry and Fire Protection provides fire protection for approximately 31 million acres of privately owned timber, range, and brushland. It also contracts with the federal government and 31 California counties to provide fire protection in designated

STATE WATER PROJECT

△ CITIES

Figure 10.2

areas for which they are responsible.

The department regulates timber harvesting on private forestland, operates 44 conservation camps, offers technical and financial assistance to landowners for forest and land management, and supervises seven state forests and three tree nurseries.

The *State Board of Forestry*, which has nine members appointed by the governor to four-year terms, gives policy guidance to the department.

DEPARTMENT OF PARKS AND RECREATION

The Department of Parks and Recreation manages more than one million acres in the state park system, which consists of 278 units in parks, reserves, historical sites, recreation areas, beaches, wayside campgrounds, wilderness areas, underwater parks, and off-highway vehicle areas and trails.

The department also administers federal and state grants for state, regional, and local park and open-space areas. In recent years, state bond sales have been a major source of funding local assistance grants, as well as state park facilities. California's growing population is predominantly urban, and increased emphasis is being given to recreational facilities in or near metropolitan areas.

The *California State Park and Recreation Commission* advises the department on proposed state park system projects and operating policies. The commission's nine members are appointed by the governor to three-year terms.

The *Off-Highway Vehicle Recreation Commission,* with seven members, sets policies for the department's development and operation of vehicular recreation areas and trails.

The *State Historical Resources Commission,* consisting of nine members, is responsible for the identification, preservation, and enhancement of cultural resources throughout California as set forth in the National Historic Preservation Act.

THE DEPARTMENT OF FISH AND GAME

The Department of Fish and Game is responsible for protecting, managing, and enhancing fish, wildlife, and native plant resources. Its functions include protection and propagation of fish and wildlife, review of environmental impact reports, and enforcement of hunting and fishing regulations. Department funds come principally from hunting and fishing licenses, a special tax on commercial fishing, and federal aid.

The *Fish and Game Commission,* one of the few commissions established by the state constitution, sets policies for the Department of Fish and Game. Its five members are appointed by the governor to six-year terms. The commission also regulates fishing and hunting, under authority granted by the legislature.

The *Wildlife Conservation Board* acquires property to protect and preserve wildlife and to provide facilities for fishing, hunting, and recreational access. Its activities are principally financed by voter-approved bond acts and state horse racing revenues. This revenue is used to acquire land and develop facilities. Most public access facilities financed through the Wildlife Conservation Board are operated by local governments. Projects include wildlife areas, ecological reserves, and access routes to fishing and hunting areas.

DEPARTMENT OF BOATING AND WATERWAYS

The Department of Boating and Waterways constructs boating facilities in state parks and at State Water Project reservoir. It makes loans to public and private marina operators for development of small craft harbors and marinas, as well as grants to local agencies for boat launching facilities, boating safety, and law enforcement. It also coordinates the state's beach erosion control program. The department has a seven-member advisory commission whose members are appointed by the governor to four-year terms.

DEPARTMENT OF CONSERVATION

The Department of Conservation has responsibility for programs relating to California's petroleum, geothermal, mineral, soil resources, and recycling of natural resources.

The *Oil and Gas* **division** regulates the development, operation, maintenance, and abandonment of oil and gas wells, including off-shore wells in state waters (up to three miles off shore), in addition to geothermal wells.

The *Mines and Geology* **division** classifies designated lands according to their mineral content and directs a farmland mapping program. It also measures earthquakes through its strong-motion instrumentation program. The *State Mining and Geology Board,* with nine members appointed by the governor to four-year terms, gives policy direction to this division for surface mining and reclamation practice, as well as for the conservation and development of mineral resources.

The *Land Conservation* **unit** administers the provisions of the *Williamson Act,* which encourages the preservation of open space and agricultural lands. Under this program the state provides partial reimbursement to cities and counties for tax revenue losses resulting from reduced assessments on land restricted to agricultural and open-space uses.

The *Recycling* **division** administers the provisions of the California Beverage Container Recycling and Litter Reduction Act (AB 2020) enacted in 1986. The Act ensures convenient and economic recycling opportunities of beverage containers on a statewide level. The Beverage Container Recycling Advisory Committee, composed of 12 appointed members, was created under the provisions of AB 2020 to advise the director of the department on all issues concerning the recycling of beverage containers in California.

CALIFORNIA CONSERVATION CORPS

The California Conservation Corps is a program for young men and women between the ages of 18 and 23. Its aim is to conserve and enhance the state's natural resources, while offering youth on-the-job training, work experience, and educational skills. CCC members provide emergency fire-fighting and natural disaster relief services and work on public service projects relating to resource management and conservation. Projects are undertaken for local, state, and federal agencies and nonprofit organizations and must meet the Corps' conservation guidelines.

Working with community colleges, the Conservation Corps offers classes to improve reading and writing skills, develop conservation awareness, and encourage employment opportunities. It has 16 residential centers, more than 20 nonresidential satellite facilities, and a training academy.

STATE LANDS COMMISSION

The State Lands Commission is an independent body within the Resources Agency composed of the state controller, the lieutenant governor, and the director of finance. The commission manages four million acres of lands which the state has received from the federal government. These lands include coastal tide and submerged lands, beds of navigable rivers and lakes, and vacant lands which were granted by Congress for support of schools. The commission may approve the use of state lands if the use is consistent with the public interest. It may lease land under its control for the extraction of oil, gas, geothermal, and mineral resources. Other responsibilities include classification of lands according to their possible use, development of regulations to assure their protection, administration of tideland trusts granted by the legislature, determination of the boundaries of state-owned lands, and the maintenance of appropriate records for lands and resources under the commission's jurisdiction.

CALIFORNIA ENERGY COMMISSION

The California Energy Commission (whose official title is the Energy Resources and Development Commission) is the state's principal energy planning organization.

The commission has five major areas of responsibility: forecasting future statewide electricity needs, licensing power plants sufficient to meet those needs, promoting conservation, developing renewable energy resources and alternative energy-generating technologies and clean-transportation fuel technologies, and planning for and directing state response to energy emergencies. The commission has five divisions to carry out these responsibilities: Forecasting and Planning, Siting and Environmental, Energy Efficiency and Local Assistance, Energy Technology Development, and Administrative Services.

The commission forecasts future energy trends every two years through a biennial report called the California Energy Plan. The report provides the basis for California's energy policy and makes five-, 12-, and 20-year projections of state growth and energy needs.

CALIFORNIA TAHOE CONSERVANCY

The California Tahoe Conservancy, established in 1984, is the lead agency in implementing the $85 million Tahoe Bond Act of 1982. It is authorized to acquire and improve environmentally sensitive lands in the Lake Tahoe Basin and other undeveloped lands threatened with development, including lands located within stream environment zones and those providing lakeshore access to the public, preservation of wildlife habitat, or a combination of benefits.

The conservancy has broad powers to establish its own acquisition policies and site improvement, make grants to nonprofit organizations and to state, federal, and local agencies for buying property, and to manage and lease lands acquired with bond proceeds.

COLORADO RIVER BOARD OF CALIFORNIA

The ten-member Colorado River Board of California is responsible for protecting California's rights and interests in the water and power resources of the Colorado River. The Colorado River Basin, a 244,000 square-mile area comprising portions of seven states and northwestern Mexico, is an important source of hydroelectric power for California and has furnished about 65 percent of the water used in southern California. Because of a court decision awarding more Colorado River water to Arizona, California will receive a smaller share of this water in the future. The board represents the state in working with the other basin states and federal agencies and seeks legislative, court, and administrative decisions that protect the state's interests.

CALIFORNIA COASTAL COMMISSION

The California Coastal Commission is responsible for administering the state's coastal management program in accord with the amended 1976 Coastal Act. The 1976 law declares that the coast is a state resource to be protected through the cooperative efforts of state and local governments. It set policies for uses of a defined coastal zone, including public access, development, land and water use, natural resources, energy, transportation, recreation, and agriculture.

The two principal elements of the coastal management program involve the preparation of local coastal programs (LCPs) and the regulation of development within the coastal zone. Following certification of local coastal programs by the state commission, authority to issue most permits for development rests with local governments subject to certain appeals to the commission. Permits from the state commission are required for development of tidelands, submerged lands, or public trust lands (e.g., placement of piers, off shore oil and gas development in state jurisdiction, and filling of wetlands) and public works projects.

The Coastal Commission assists local governments in their enforcement of permit requirements, hears permit appeals, studies proposed amendments to local plans, and reviews entire plans at least once every five years for conformity with state policies. The commission also monitors energy development in the coastal zone and is required to designate areas inappropriate for power plants.

In addition, the Coastal Commission is the designated state coastal management agency for purposes of administering the federal Coastal Zone Management Act within California. The Act gives the commission substantial authority over federally sponsored, funded or licensed activities, and activities on federal lands and waters, including offshore oil development. Under this act California also has received substantial federal funding to develop and implement the federally certified California Coastal Management Program.

The commission has 15 members, consisting of six public members, six elected local officials, and three non-voting ex-officio members representing state agencies. The members may also have alternates. The commission is required to coordinate its activities with state departments and other commissions whose responsibilities also affect the coast, especially the California Coastal Conservancy and the San Francisco Bay Conservation and Development Commission. It also sponsors an award-winning education and public involvement program.

CALIFORNIA COASTAL CONSERVANCY

The California Coastal Conservancy is authorized to acquire land, undertake projects, and award grants to preserve agricultural land and significant coastal resources and to consolidate subdivided land. Its projects also include the restorations of wetlands, marshes, and other natural resources, development of a system of public accessways, and the improvement of coastal urban land uses, such as waterfronts. The conservancy also recommends certain urban waterfront projects for revenue bond financing.

The Coastal Conservancy resolves coastal land use and resource conflicts that are not amenable to solution through regulatory processes. It works with local governments to implement their local coastal programs (LCPs). The conservancy's jurisdiction coincides with the coastal zone boundaries set for the California Coastal Commission and also includes San Francisco Bay and the Suisun Marsh.

The conservancy's governing board consists of the secretary of the Resources Agency, the Coastal Commission chair, the director of finance, and four public members appointed to four-year terms. This board must approve all conservancy projects, which are required to conform to California Coastal Act policies.

SAN FRANCISCO BAY CONSERVATION AND DEVELOPMENT COMMISSION

The San Francisco Bay Conservation and Development Commission is a regional special purpose commission responsible for updating and implementing the San Francisco Bay Plan. Created in 1965, it has regulatory authority over dredging and filling of the bay and over changing the uses of adjacent salt ponds and managed wetlands of the land within 100 feet of the shore. BCDC also implements and updates the Suisun Marsh Protection Plan, regulating land uses within the 89,000 acres of the marsh. The commission may amend the San Francisco Bay Plan by a two-thirds vote of its 27 members, who represent federal, state and local governments and the general public.

OTHER REGIONAL BODIES

Two regional bodies not a part of the Resources Agency implement resource programs and plans in the state:

The *Tahoe Regional Planning Agency* was created under a compact enacted by the California and Nevada legislatures and ratified by Congress in 1969. The compact was extensively amended in 1980.

The TRPA governing board was charged with setting "environmental threshold carrying capacities" for the Tahoe region—standards for such elements as air and water quality, soil conservation, and noise. In April 1984, on the basis of these standards, the TRPA board adopted a new regional plan for land use, transportation, conservation of scenic and other natural resources, recreation and public services, and facilities.

The 1984 TRPA regional plan was challenged by several lawsuits, however, including a suit filed by California's attorney general, questioning the adequacy of the plan's provisions. As a result, in June 1984 a preliminary injunction essentially halted TRPA's issuance of building permits for new development. Consensus talks held over the next three years resulted in settlement of litigation and adoption of a new TRPA regional Plan in 1987. New construction resumed in 1986.

The Regional Plan contains several documents: Goals and Policies, Code of Ordinances, Plan Area Statements, "208" Water Quality Plan, Regional Transportation/Air Quality Plan, and Capital Financing Plan.

The TRPA Governing Board has 15 members. California and Nevada each have three representatives of local governments within the region and four members who live outside the region. The California delegation includes two members appointed by the governor, one appointed by the Assembly speaker and one appointed by the Senate Rules Committee. The fifteenth member is a non-voting appointee of the President of the United States.

The *Santa Monica Mountains Conservancy* purchases land and provides grants to state and local agencies and nonprofit corporations to implement the Santa Monica Mountains Comprehensive Plan. The conservancy is authorized to acquire and improve open space lands for preservation and public recreation use, create buffer zones surrounding federal and state park sites, restore natural resources areas, and design and implement park and trail improvements. The conservancy has a board of seven voting members and is scheduled to go out of existence July 1, 1995, unless extended by legislation.

ENVIRONMENTAL PROTECTION AGENCY

The California Environmental Protection Agency was established in July 1991, replacing the Environmental Affairs agency. Cal-EPA unifies the state's environmental authority under a single accountable, cabinet-level agency. In general the objectives of the Cal-EPA focus on better coordination and prioritization of the state's efforts to protect the environment with an emphasis on regulatory enforcement.

There are three areas within Cal-EPA at the agency level:

Hazardous Substance Cleanup Arbitration Panel. This panel promotes the cleanup of hazardous waste sites on the California Superfund List by arbitrating disputes over cleanup cost liability.

Registration of Environmental Assessors. Cal-EPA encourages the voluntary registration of environmental assessors and the use of registered assessors to achieve higher degrees of compliance and environmental laws.

Hazardous Materials Data Management. This office provides a variety of products and services intended to make it easier to obtain and assemble toxic-related information from a wide range of sources.

The Secretary of the California Environmental Protection Agency serves in the governor's cabinet, reporting on activities of the Air Resources Board, the California Integrated Waste Management Board, the Departments of Pesticide Regulation and Toxic Substances Control, the Office of Environmental Health Hazard Assessment and the State Water Resources Control Board.

AIR RESOURCES BOARD
The Air Resources Board sets California's motor vehicle emissions

---

ENVIRONMENTAL PROTECTION AGENCY (Cal-EPA)

Air Resources Board	Department of Toxic Substances
California Integrated Waste	Control
Management Board	Office of Environmental Health
Department of Pesticide	Hazard Assessment
Regulation	State Water Resources Control Board

Figure 10.3

for controlling air pollution. Those standards are distinct from those set by the federal EPA and are typically the nation's strictest. The board, composed of a full-time chairperson and eight part-time members appointed by the governor, sets the ambient air quality standards for the state.

The ARB also monitors air quality and administers the nation's second largest research air pollution program, which conducts studies on topics as diverse as health and crop damage, atmospheric science and new technology.

ARB provides financial support and technical expertise to help county and regional pollution control officials set emission limits for industrial causes of air pollution, and develops local clean air plans. The ARB also helps these agencies enforce local pollution control rules by providing technical staff or highly sophisticated testing equipment when needed. In addition to setting emission standards, the board adopts certification test procedures and conducts follow-up, assembly-line, and random sampling tests to ensure that production vehicles meet the same emission levels as prototype vehicles used in certification tests. The program is operated by the Bureau of Automotive Repair.

The ARB also maintains its own, independent enforcement program. This effort ensures that statewide air quality rules are met, such as those governing the make-up of fuels or limiting motor vehicle emissions.

In cooperation with 33 county or regional air pollution control districts (APCDs), the ARB regulates emissions from non-automotive or stationary sources of pollution such as factories, oil refineries, and power plants.

Local districts are either county or regional in scope. A county APCD is governed by the board of supervisors.

The *Bay Area Air Quality Management District* has jurisdiction in all or portions of the nine counties within the San Francisco Bay Area Air Basin. Its 18-member board is composed of supervisors and city council members of the participating counties.

The *South Coast Air Quality Management District* includes all or portions of four counties in the South Coast Basin. Its 14-member board is composed of 11 supervisors and city council members and three public members appointed by the governor, the Senate Rules Committee, and the speaker of the Assembly. State law also permits the formation of a "unified" APCD by two or more counties within an air basin. At present there are unified districts in the North Central Coast Air Basin and Great Basin Valleys Air Basin.

State law requires formation of a Basin Coordinating Council within any air basin containing two or more local districts. Each council includes one representative from each APCD in the basin.

CALIFORNIA'S AIR POLLUTION CONTROL AND AIR QUALITY MANAGEMENT DISTRICTS

Figure 10.4

CALIFORNIA INTEGRATED WASTE MANAGEMENT BOARD

The California Integrated Waste Management Board implements laws to advance the technologies and handling practices of non-hazardous solid waste disposal in the state. The board also encourages adoption of alternative waste disposal practices, such as recycling and conversion to energy, that are environmentally, economically, and technically sound. The CIWMB staff carries out its responsibilities through three divisions.

The Planning and Assistance division deals with the development of local plans to implement the waste diversion goals required of cities and counties.

The Permitting and Compliance division ensures that state integrated waste programs are effectively implemented at the local level by working cooperatively with the Local Enforcement Agencies (LEA).

The Research and Technology Development division is the primary research arm of the board.

The board has nine members, seven of whom are appointed by the governor and one each by the speaker of the Assembly and the president pro tempore of the Senate.

DEPARTMENT OF PESTICIDE REGULATION

The California Department of Pesticide Regulation enforces all laws governing the use of pesticides in California, whether it be in agriculture, industry, business or the home.

Under the direction and supervision of the Department of Pesticide Regulation, the county agricultural commissioners carry out pesticide enforcement activities at the local level.

The department is comprised of six branches: Pesticide Registration; Medical Toxicology; Worker Health and Safety; Environmental Monitoring and Pest Management; Pesticide Use Enforcement, and Information Services.

DEPARTMENT OF TOXIC SUBSTANCES CONTROL

The mission of the Department of Toxic Substances is to protect and enhance public health and the environment by regulating the management of hazardous waste and promoting the reduction of such waste.

The department is responsible for implementing and enforcing provisions of the state's Hazardous Waste Control Act, the Hazardous Substances Account Act, and pursuant regulations. This authority is based in the Health and Safety Code and the California Code of Regulations.

THE OFFICE OF ENVIRONMENTAL HEALTH HAZARD ASSESSMENT

The Office of Environmental Health Hazard Assessment provides scientific and technical expertise assessing the human health risks of chemicals in the environment. OEHHA's primary role is as risk assessor for various programs under the California Environmental Protection Agency (Cal-EPA), as well as other state and local agencies.

STATE WATER RESOURCES CONTROL BOARD

The State Water Resources Control Board regulates California's water quality and allocates water rights. Created in 1967 by the legislature, the five-member board protects and regulates the quality of surface, ground and coastal waters. The five full-time members are appointed by the governor to serve four-year terms. Its programs and policies are designed to protect all beneficial uses of California water including domestic, municipal, agricultural and industrial supply, power generation, recreation, aesthetic enjoyment, navigation, and preservation and enhancement of fish and wildlife.

To accomplish these tasks, the board, in conjunction with nine Regional Water Quality Control Boards, conducts planning, research, and monitoring programs, as well as regulatory oversight for the state's waters. The board sets policy for and has statutory authority to review most actions of the nine regional boards. The state board also adopts a single budget for the state and regional boards. Each regional board has nine part-time, unsalaried members, also appointed by the governor to four-year terms. Appeals from regional board actions are heard and decided upon by the state board.

State Water Resources Control Board programs include:

Water quality. State and regional boards carry out state policies by developing water pollution control programs, implementing ground water protection laws and working to ensure prevention, cleanup and containment. These programs include the Toxics Clean Up Act; Waste Disposal to Land; Solid Waste Disposal, and Underground Storage Tanks. Board responsibilities also include coastal water protection with activities including research, monitoring and regulatory oversight.

Water rights. The state board issues permits for water rights specifying amounts, conditions and construction timetables for diversion and storage. These "rights" are permits to appropriate water from surface rivers, streams, and lakes.

Loans and grants. Since 1972 the state board has assisted the federal Environmental Protection Agency in administering the multi-billion dollar Clean Water Grants program in California to finance construction of municipal sewage treatment facilities. In 1987, Congress reauthorized the Clean Water Act and created state revolving loan programs capitalized in part by federal funds.

11

STATE AND CONSUMER SERVICES AGENCY

The State and Consumer Services Agency provides administrative and supportive services to otherwise unrelated units of state government. Some of these units are completely independent, but through the agency's secretary their concerns and points of view are represented at the cabinet level.

STATE AND CONSUMER SERVICES AGENCY

State Personnel Board	Department of General Services
Public Employees' Retirement System	Department of Veterans Affairs
State Teachers' Retirement System	Department of Fair Employment and Housing
Franchise Tax Board	State Fire Marshal
Department of Consumer Affairs	Museum of Science and Industry

Figure 11.1

PERSONNEL-RELATED UNITS

To protect employees from being hired or fired on the basis of political considerations rather than ability and experience, most positions in state government are regulated by a personnel management system called civil service. In 1992, there were 154,000 civil service employees in California.

STATE PERSONNEL BOARD

Since 1984 there have been two central personnel agencies regulating the state civil service system. The state Personnel Board, established by the constitution, oversees the appointment and promotion process. It consists of five members appointed by the governor and confirmed by the Senate.

The Department of Personnel Administration, established in 1984, is part of the executive branch of state government. It has assumed many of the responsibilities previously held by the Personnel Board. The DPA regulates wages, benefits, and working conditions and represents the management point of view in collective bargaining with state employee groups.

Appointments. The role of the Personnel Board is to ensure a fair and efficient selection of job applicants and employees in all departments through its centralized regulations.

The recruiting and examining program is based on the belief that a competitive job-related selection ensures the state will have the best employees. Each job is studied and classified according to its duties and responsibilities and the skills and expertise required. There are about 4,000 different classes of employment in state government. A variety of testing techniques may be employed, including written examinations to determine the applicant's knowledge and ability; interviews to appraise education, experience, and relevant personality traits; performance tests of applicable manual skills; and medical examinations to ensure that the applicant meets physical standards.

The examination and appointment process is largely decentralized with individualized departments conducting their own civil service examinations according to Personnel Board regulations.

The board also serves as an appeals board when employees believe that serious disciplinary action is unjustified or when employees believe they were discriminated against or otherwise treated in violation of Personnel Board laws and rules. The board also provides guidance and monitors departmental affirmative action programs.

To give the political heads of agencies some flexibility in selecting civil servants for high level policy-influencing positions, the civil service system has a career executive category which includes most of the very highest ranking positions. These positions are unusual in that the civil servant occupying a career executive position may be removed without cause, often as administrations or supervising authorities change. The removed employee may then revert to his or her previous civil service position.

Salaries and benefits. State civil service employees and employees of school districts, the California State University, and the University of California negotiate salaries, benefits, and working conditions through the collective bargaining process. Employees choose their own bargaining representatives to represent them in negotiations. The management point of view is represented by the Department of Personnel Administration, a part of the executive branch.

The Public Employment Relations Board (PERB) supervises and regulates the bargaining process. It decides what constitutes appropriate employee bargaining units, conducts elections to determine employee representatives, establishes and oversees negotiating procedures, and tries to prevent or remedy unfair practices by either employer or employee. The board's responsibilities include informing the public about negotiations and monitoring the financial affairs of employee organizations. The five members of the board are appointed to five-year terms by the governor. They serve full time and receive an annual salary.

Non-civil service employees. The state civil service system includes every officer and employee of the state except those expressly exempted by the constitution. These exempt employees are primarily high level officials, including department heads, board and commission members, and others whose work is directly involved with policy formation. They are appointed by elected officials or by persons immediately responsible to those officials. The appointing authority determines their competence and performance.

The largest exempt categories include persons employed by the legislature and the judiciary. Elected officials, officials appointed by the governor, and members of boards and commissions are also exempt, as are employees of the offices of governor and lieutenant governor. Typically these officials are allowed to appoint one or two additional exempt persons.

While not a part of state civil service, the employees of state educational institutions have their own personnel systems.

RETIREMENT AND BENEFIT SYSTEMS

Almost all public employees in the state are covered under either a state or local retirement system. The *Public Employees' Retirement System*, an independent agency, administers a program that provides retirement and health benefits to all state employees. The costs of these benefits are shared by employer and employee. PERS also covers all non-teaching employees of school districts, people employed by public agencies (i.e. utility companies), and many employees of the California State University and the University of California. It administers the retirement systems for legislators and judges and the Social Security program for all public agencies in the state. The *State Teachers' Retirement System*, a separate agency, administers the retirement program which covers all certificated public school employees from kindergarten through community college.

Some cities and counties provide their own retirement and benefit systems; others purchase these services from the state. In 1992, contracting agencies included 410 cities, 36 counties, four school districts, and 720 special districts.

PERS makes medical and hospital insurance available, at the individual's option, to all state workers covered by state retirement programs. Cities, counties, and local districts that contract for the retirement program may choose to offer this health coverage as well.

OTHER AGENCY UNITS

The State and Consumer Services Agency also includes several units that provide varying administrative and supportive services to other government agencies and the public.

FRANCHISE TAX BOARD

The primary role of the Franchise Tax Board is to collect state taxes which are based on income. It collects personal income taxes and bank and corporation taxes and audits these tax returns. It also administers a property tax relief program for senior citizens and audits campaign finance reports as required by the Political Reform Act of 1974. The board provides free taxpayer assistance through toll-free telephone lines and 16 walk-in centers throughout the state. The board is composed of three officers: the state controller, the director of finance, and the chairman of the Board of Equalization.

DEPARTMENT OF CONSUMER AFFAIRS

The Department of Consumer Affairs is responsible for promoting consumer awareness and for protecting the public from fraudulent business practices and incompetent service. The department oversees 41 boards and bureaus which are responsible for setting training and other standards for various professions and occupations, including public accountants, beauty operators, engineers, architects, contractors, boxers, registered nurses, and funeral directors. The boards grant licenses and may suspend or revoke them. The members of these boards are appointed by the governor; a majority of members must represent the public.

The department also administers statewide consumer protection activities, which include processing complaints, evaluating proposed legislation of consumer interest, and issuing informational material.

DEPARTMENT OF GENERAL SERVICES

The Department of General Services is the state's business manager with responsibilities which include planning, acquisition, construction, maintenance and police protection of state buildings and property; architectural services; purchasing, printing, administrative and contract services; telecommunications; and transportation management.

Because of its business oversight functions, the Department of General Services is also represented on many state boards, commissions and committees which perform various tasks such as the allocation of bond monies for the building and rehabilitation of schools and adjudication of claims for the State of California.

By meeting these varied responsibilities for centralized management review, control, and support, the department seeks to increase effectiveness and economy in the administration of state government and to maintain responsive working relationships with client agencies.

CALIFORNIA DEPARTMENT OF VETERANS AFFAIRS

The California Department of Veterans Affairs helps veterans and their dependents obtain federal and state benefits. It operates the Veterans Home of California which serves as a residence, residential health care facility, and hospital in Yountville. The department also administers the Cal-Vet farm and home loan program, a self-supporting program which uses state bond revenues to enable veterans to buy homes, condominiums, townhouses, mobile homes, or farms at lower than conventional interest rates.

DEPARTMENT OF FAIR EMPLOYMENT AND HOUSING

The Department of Fair Employment and Housing enforces The Fair Employment and Housing Act and other regulations which protect Californians from discrimination in employment and housing on the basis of race, color, religion, national origin, sex, marital status, age, or physical disability. If the department determines a discrimination complaint is valid and conciliation efforts have failed, it refers the matter to the independent Fair Employment and Housing Commission, which conducts public hearings and issues a decision. The seven members of the commission are appointed by the governor to four-year terms; they serve part time and do not receive a salary.

OFFICE OF THE STATE FIRE MARSHAL

The Fire Marshal works to prevent loss of life and property from fire. This office prepares, adopts, and enforces minimum fire safety building standards and standards for fabrics, fireworks, fire extinguishers, explosives, and hazardous liquid pipelines. It collects and analyzes data on all fires and investigates fires when arson is suspected.

MUSEUM OF SCIENCE AND INDUSTRY

The Museum of Science and Industry, a state-owned educational, civic, and recreational center in Los Angeles, offers programs and exhibits in the fields of science, health, and economics. A second state-owned facility, the Museum of Afro-American History and Culture, is located on the same site. Both museums are administered by boards of directors appointed by the governor.

12

YOUTH AND ADULT CORRECTIONAL AGENCY

The Youth and Adult Correctional Agency oversees the administration of all California correctional departments and programs and provides a consistent, coordinated state policy regarding future institutional needs, programs, and legislation for both adult and youthful offenders.

Persons convicted of felonies may be imprisoned in state correctional institutions. Those convicted of misdemeanors or lesser felonies serve their time in county detention facilities with sentences of up to one year. Of the total number of people convicted of felonies in California, about 20 percent go into the state system, 67 percent into county facilities. Most of the remainder serve their time on probation. Crimes that result in federal prosecution, such as smuggling, immigration law violation, or counterfeiting are handled by the federal judicial system and confinement in federal prisons.

DEPARTMENT OF CORRECTIONS

The Department of Corrections holds responsibility for incarcerating California's criminal offenders. It also provides parole services including supervision, surveillance, and specialized services for parolees as they transition from prison to the community. The Department of Corrections is the largest department under the Youth and Adult Correctional Agency. The department director is appointed by the governor to manage the state's prison, parole, and community-based correctional systems.

YOUTH AND ADULT CORRECTIONAL AGENCY

Department of Corrections	Youthful Offender Parole Board
Board of Prison Terms	Board of Corrections
Prison Industry Authority	Department of the Youth Authority

Figure 12.1

CDC is divided into six divisions: Institutions; Paroles and Community Service; Planning and Construction; Administrative Services; Evaluation and Compliance, and Legal Affairs.

The largest division is the *Institutions* division, which manages 22 state prisons housing minimum to maximum security custody inmates. These prisons include psychiatric facilities and a drug treatment center for narcotic addicts under civil commitment. The department also operates 41 conservation camps, which house minimum security custody inmates who perform various forest conservation and fire prevention functions and complete thousands of hours of community service work. Four camps operate in cooperation with the Department of Forestry; four in cooperation with Los Angeles County.

Prisons are small cities averaging about 4,000 inmates and staff. Inmates are provided with employment and academic opportunities as well as a variety of substance abuse programs. Three prisons also operate hospitals licensed by the California Department of Health.

In 1980, approximately 24,000 inmates were in state prisons and camps; by 1991, there were more than 101,500 inmates housed by the Department of Corrections. Projected forecasts indicate California's prison population will reach 140,000 by 1997. In 1992, the average yearly cost to house an inmate was $20,927.

The *Paroles and Community Service* division is responsible for 56 Community Correctional facilities (CCFs) and the supervision of more than 83,000. The division provides parolee programs for literacy training, substance abuse treatment, and employment placement. There are 135 parole offices in 79 locations throughout California. In 1992, the average yearly cost to supervise a parolee was $2,439.

The *Planning and Construction* division handles all financial issues concerning new prison construction. The division is also responsible for contracts management, construction procurement, legislative analysis and development, and special projects.

The *Administrative Services* division delivers the services that keep the wheels of CDC turning. ASD provides support to the entire department in fiscal and personnel management, training, facilities planning and business services.

The *Evaluation and Compliance* division analyzes departmental systems and makes recommendations for improvements.

The *Legal Affairs* division serves as counsel to the CDC, administers the second-level review of all outstanding construction claims, and initiates the department's legal defense in arbitration for claims that cannot be resolved. The division is divided into three separate units: Correctional Law, Claims Review, and Arbitration Defense.

Reception centers are currently allied to eight institutions. These centers provide diagnostic classification evaluations of convicted felons awaiting sentencing and will, upon request, make sentencing recommendations to the courts. When individuals are committed to prison, these centers compile personal histories that help determine

CALIFORNIA STATE PRISONS

Department of Corrections

♦ Original Prisons (Pre-1982)
1. California State Prison, San Quentin
2. California State Prison, Old Folsom
3. California Institution for Men
4. Correctional Training Facility
5. California Institution for Women
6. Deuel Vocational Institution
7. California Men's Colony
8. California Correctional Institution
9. California Medical Facility
10. California Rehabilitation Center
11. California Correctional Center
12. Sierra Conservation Center

■ New Prisons Constructed
1. California Medical Facility – South
2. Southern Maximum Security Complex
3. California State Prison, New Folsom
4. Northern California Women's Facility
5. Richard J. Donovan Correctional Facility at Rock Mountain
6. Avenal State Prison
7. Mule Creek State Prison
8. California State Prison, Corcoran
9. Chuckawalla Valley State Prison
10. Pelican Bay State Prison

● Under Construction
1. Central California Women's Facility
2. California State Prison, Kern County (Wasco)
3. California State Prison, Kern County (Delano)
4. California State Prison, Imperial County (North)

▲ Proposed New Prisons
1. California Reception Center, Los Angeles County
2. California State Prison, Los Angeles County
3. California State Prison, Fresno County (Coalinga)
4. California State Prison, Imperial County (South)
5. San Quentin Joint Use Correctional Facility
6. California State Prison, Lassen County II
7. California State Prison, Riverside County II
8. California State Prison, Madera County II (Women)

(Source: Department of Corrections)

Figure 12.2

suitable custody and program needs. New male prisoners are processed through reception centers at San Quentin, Chino, Tracy, Vacaville, San Diego, Wasco, or Delano. New female prisoners are processed through reception centers in Stockton at the Northern California Women's Facility (NCWF) or Corona at the California Institute for Women (CIW).

Each institution is headed by a warden and has its own administrative staff. Institutional operations are divided into custody and program functions. Major programs at the institutions include 31 correctional industry operations and seven agricultural enterprises. For example, four institutions have extensive dairy operations; Deuel Vocational Institution operates a furniture and mattress factory; and Folsom Prison manufactures automobile license plates. These industries provide work opportunities in addition to the normal support and maintenance jobs. Inmates are paid on the basis of skills, production, and hours worked.

The institutions also provide vocational training and academic instruction ranging from literacy classes to college correspondence courses, as well as group and individual counseling.

BOARD OF PRISON TERMS

The Board of Prison Terms serves as the state parole board. The board's primary function is to consider parole release for persons sentenced to prison with a term of life imprisonment with the possibility of parole. It reviews information concerning the crime, prior criminal history, and what the inmate has done in prison to prepare for future release. Additionally, the board determines whether and for how long a parolee should be returned to prison for a violation of parole; reviews non-life sentences to determine that specific sentences conform to those received by inmates convicted of similar offenses; and advises the governor regarding clemency matters.

All other incarcerated felons serve a set term as established by the legislature and imposed by the court. They cannot be held longer than the term imposed; however, they may reduce the period of time spent in prison by receiving credit for good behavior or participation in a work program. Persons sentenced to determinate and indeterminate terms of imprisonment are subject to the jurisdiction of the board following their release on parole.

The Board of Prison Terms has nine full-time commissioners appointed by the governor, one of which is selected as the chair. All appointees must receive Senate confirmation. Each commissioner serves a four-year term and upon completion of the term may be reappointed.

DEPARTMENT OF THE YOUTH AUTHORITY

The Department of the Youth Authority, established in 1941, provides institutional training and parole supervision for juvenile and young adult offenders. CYA is the largest youthful offender agency in the nation with about 8,300 young men and women in institutions and camps, and approximately 5,800 on parole. The department requires offenders to become accountable for illegal behavior, and provides training programs.

In general, 18 years is the dividing age between adult and juvenile offenders. Recent changes in the law prohibit the Youth Authority from accepting serious felony offenders who are 18 or older at the time of the offense. Recent law also makes it possible for offenders as young as 16 to have their cases handled in adult criminal court if certain serious felonies are committed, and to be sentenced to the Department of Corrections rather than to the Youth Authority.

The Youth Authority's jurisdiction for most serious felony offenders, both juvenile and young adult, ends on the offender's twenty-fifth birthday. Direct commitments to the Youth Authority are indeterminate periods which may not exceed adult sentences for the same offenses.

The *Parole Services and Community Corrections* **branch** supervises offenders released to the community. The branch is responsible for monitoring juvenile halls, camps and ranches, jails and lockups, and annually inspecting these facilities. To provide maximum public protection, Community Corrections works closely with law enforcement agencies, probation departments, and the courts to maintain and improve the juvenile justice system.

Parole Services also staffs two intensive drug treatment programs for parolees who have drug and alcohol problems but have not committed criminal acts. The branch is divided administratively into two regions, with a staff of field parole agents working out of 32 parole offices throughout the state.

The *Institutions and Camps* **branch** operates 11 institutions (including two reception centers-clinics), four rural conservation camps, and two institution-based camps used for pre-release training. Offenders committed to the CYA are screened and tested at the reception centers before being assigned to a permanent program. Varied education and job training programs are offered, and wards are becoming increasingly involved in public service programs in the community. Firefighting, conservation, and other vocational training programs are offered in the conservation camps.

YOUTHFUL OFFENDER PAROLE BOARD

The Youthful Offender Parole Board is the paroling authority for young persons committed by the courts to the Department of the Youth Authority. The board has seven members appointed by the governor to four-year terms. Appointments are subject to Senate confirmation.

The board functions under a modified indeterminate sentencing structure and has sole authority to order and set conditions for parole, revoke or suspend parole, recommend treatment and training programs, return nonresidents to the jurisdiction of their home states, return cases to the committing court for alternate disposition, and to discharge commitments from jurisdiction. In carrying out these functions and authorities, the board conducts over 20,000 hearings annually throughout the state.

BOARD OF CORRECTIONS

The Board of Corrections sets minimum standards for health care, programs, procedures and construction of local detention facilities. It has statutory responsibility for establishing selection criteria and training standards for local probation and corrections officers, and subvenes costs incurred by counties in meeting training standards. The board also has responsibility for administering the County Correctional Facility Capital Expenditure Fund, a program that allocates nearly $1.5 billion for county jail construction, and for the development of a statewide bond program for joint state-local facilities for substance abusers.

PRISON INDUSTRY AUTHORITY

The Prison Industry Authority and its governing body, the Prison Industry Board, operates a variety of manufacturing, construction, agricultural, and service industries on prison grounds. The PIA program employs approximately 8,000 inmates and is funded by revenue generated from the sale of products and services.

YOUTH AUTHORITY INSTITUTIONS AND CAMPS

Ben Lomond	Ben Lomond Conservation Camp
Camarillo	Ventura School
Ione	Preston School of Industry
Mariposa	Mt. Bullion Conservation Camp
Nevada City	Washington Ridge Conservation Camp
Norwalk	Southern Reception Center-Clinic
Ontario	Heman G. Stark Training School
Paso Robles	El Paso de Robles School
Pine Grove	Pine Grove Conservation Camp
Sacramento	Northern Reception Center-Clinic
Stockton	O.H. Close School
Stockton	N.A. Chaderjian
Stockton	Karl Holton School
Stockton	Dewitt Nelson Training Center
Whittier	Fred C. Nelles School

Figure 12.3

13

OTHER DEPARTMENTS, BOARDS, AND COMMISSIONS

The executive branch includes four cabinet-level departments and many boards and commissions created at various times to meet California's changing needs. The four departments, whose directors serve in the governor's cabinet, are independent of the major agencies.

CABINET-LEVEL DEPARTMENTS

Department of Finance	Department of Industrial Relations
Department of Food and and Agriculture	Office of Child Development and Education

Figure 13.1

DEPARTMENT OF FINANCE

The Department of Finance assists and advises the governor in the formulation of the administration's policies and programs. The department's principal functions are to supervise the development of the governor's budget, to serve as the governor's chief fiscal and policy adviser, to assure responsible and responsive state resource allocation within available resources, to foster efficient and effective state government processes, and to establish integrity in the data bases and systems of state fiscal and program performance. The department consists of the following units:

Budget Operations Support, Administrative Services, California State Accounting and Reporting System, and Fiscal Systems and Consulting. Budget Operations is responsible for providing support for the entire budgetary process, including budget planning, preparation, posting, changes, enactment, financial legislation, appropriating control accounting, and the publication of the governor's budget. *Administrative Services* provides the internal departmental activities necessary to maintain the department's daily functioning, such as personnel management, support services, business services, and training. Another unit is the *California State Accounting and Reporting System,* a computerized system of governmental and program cost accounting to be used in approximately 200 state agencies and institutions. The Fiscal Systems and Consulting unit develops and communicates fiscal and accounting policies and procedures.

Budget units. Budget preparation is performed by several departmental budget units in various program areas such as education, resources and health and welfare. Each unit is responsible for preparing a significant portion of the governor's budget to reflect the administration's policies. The responsibilities of each budget unit include generating expenditure planning estimates, analyzing and coordinating budget submissions, compiling the governor's budget and the budget bill, testifying before the legislature, and providing estimates of revenues and expenditures.

Information Technology, Financial Performance and Accountability, and Program Evaluation. The Information Technology unit monitors the acquisition and utilization of the state's electronic data processing resources, equipment, personnel, and data systems. Excluded from its control are the state legislature, the University of California, the community colleges, and the state compensation fund. Financial and Performance Accountability audits various state agencies and programs to determine financial compliance, economy and efficiency, and possible problem areas. Program Evaluation undertakes projects originating within the department, the governor's office, cabinet-level officials, or the legislature to analyze and evaluate selected state programs.

Legislation and Intergovernmental Relations and Capital Outlay. The Legislation and Intergovernmental Relations unit, in addition to performing budget unit functions, analyzes legislative bills and monitors systems created to reimburse local governments for costs mandated to them by the legislature. The Capital Outlay staff is responsible for preparation, enactment, and administration of the annual financial plan for all state capital outlay appropriations.

Public and Intergovernmental Relations. The Public and Intergovernmental Relations unit researches and responds to public inquiries regarding the governor's budget and also assists in preparing various annual publications.

DEPARTMENT OF FOOD AND AGRICULTURE

Agriculture in California is a major industry which supplies food to both domestic and export markets. As crops have become more diversified through the years, a partnership between California's government and the agricultural economy has been established to benefit both farmers and consumers. Policies to promote and protect agriculture for the present and future are developed by the Department of Food and Agriculture.

The *Division of Plant Industry* has responsibility for preventing the introduction and spread of crop pests and diseases. Its laboratories identify and classify insects, diagnose the cause of diseases in plant materials, and test seed samples for the presence of pest weeds. When harmful pests are found at new locations, the division directs the campaign to control or eradicate them. It maintains plant quarantine inspection stations near state borders on all major highways to help prevent the introduction of new plant pests.

The *Division of Animal Industry* provides protection against livestock and poultry diseases. It enforces laws regulating the quality and labeling of meat, the processing and handling of milk, and the registration and inspection of livestock to prevent cattle theft.

The *Division of Inspection Services* controls the sale and use of agricultural chemicals and inspects fruits, vegetables, nuts, eggs, and other agricultural products for quality standards.

The *Division of Measurement Standards* assists county offices of weights and measures in carrying out a program of package inspection for quality and labeling. It inspects commercially used measuring and weighing devices and enforces regulations pertaining to the quality and quantity of petroleum products including gasoline, motor oils, and brake fluid.

The *Division of Marketing Services* assists farmers and ranchers by providing crop information, production and marketing data, and reports on weather and range conditions. The division also administers the program of direct marketing from farmers to consumers.

The *State Board of Food and Agriculture* makes policy recommendations on all aspects of agriculture and often urges direct action by industry leaders and government. It advises the governor, the Department of Food and Agriculture, and, on matters regarding farm labor, the Employment Development Department. Its 15 members are appointed by the governor to four-year terms and represent a cross-section of interests from the agricultural industry, university and college systems, and the general public.

DEPARTMENT OF INDUSTRIAL RELATIONS

The Department of Industrial Relations administers and enforces state labor laws which protect the welfare of wage earners and set standards for safety, wages, hours, and working conditions.

The *Division of Workers' Compensation/Workers' Compensation Appeals Board* resolves disputed claims for compensating workers who suffer industrial injury in the course of their employment. The division also provides administrative services to assist injured workers and their employers. These services include rehabilitation plans for disabled workers and administration of the Uninsured Employers' Fund.

The *Self-Insurance Plans Unit* issues certificates of self-insurance to businesses and public agencies financially able to compensate their workers fully for industrial injuries. This program also monitors financial transactions involving these injuries.

The *State Mediation and Conciliation Service* investigates and mediates labor disputes and arranges for the selection of boards of arbitration.

The *Division of Occupational Safety and Health,* commonly referred to as Cal-DOSH, works to ensure safe and healthful working conditions for all California employees through standards enforcement, assistance to employers, occupational safety and health research, and provision of information and training. It also inspects elevators, aerial tramways, portable amusement rides, pressure vessels (i.e., boilers), and mines and tunnels.

The *Division of Labor Standards Enforcement* enforces the Industrial Welfare Commission's regulations governing 15 employment categories, such as agriculture, manufacturing, motion pictures, and more than 200 state laws regarding wages, hours, working conditions, child labor, and the licensing of farm labor contractors.

The *Division of Apprenticeship Standards* works with employer and employee groups to develop and promote apprenticeship programs for on-the-job training, and equal opportunity practices in these programs.

The *Division of Labor Statistics and Research* collects, compiles, and publishes information and statistics on economic and employment conditions in California. These include union memberships, the California Consumer Price Index (CPI), and occupational injury and illness statistics.

CHILD DEVELOPMENT AND EDUCATION

The Office of Child Development and Education was created in January 1991. The office has the responsibility of advising the governor on all issues related to child development and education, developing policies affecting children in California, and coordinating the various children's programs currently administered by 37 state-funded departments and six agencies. This includes health issues, early childhood education, child care and child development, K-12 and postsecondary education. The office will also administer the Volunteer Mentor Program.

At the time this book went to press, the authorization for the Office of Child Development and Education remained stalled in the legislature. Additionally, legislation in the Assembly has been proposed to remove the education function from this office.

BOARDS AND COMMISSIONS

Approximately 2,700 persons serve the executive branch of the state on more than 350 boards, commissions, bureaus, and councils established by law. The governor appoints a large number of these persons. The legislature also appoints many commissioners to advise it. The composition of some boards is specified by law. In other instances the appointing power is vested in designated officials with a particular concern for, or knowledge of, the matter over which the board has jurisdiction.

Some boards discharge executive functions similar to those of a department head. Others make policy and delegate administration to an executive officer. Many are regulatory, with varying degrees of administrative, legislative, and judicial power. Some boards are entirely appellate, hearing appeals from administrative decisions. A large number of boards are advisory only.

Members of most boards receive reimbursement only for actual expenses while a few full-time boards are salaried. Members of some boards and commissions are paid on a per diem basis while attending meetings.

Many boards, commissions, and councils are assigned to a department within an agency for administrative and supportive services. They are independently appointed, and the departments to which they are attached give staff service. Even such independent bodies as the state Personnel Board are assigned to an agency for purposes of communication, so that their concerns and points of view are represented at the cabinet level through the agency secretary.

Examples of several kinds of boards and commissions may illustrate the range of authority they exercise and the variety of services they render.

The *Agricultural Labor Relations Board* sets policies, procedures, and regulations to implement the Agricultural Labor Relations Act of 1975, which guarantees agricultural workers the right to bargain collectively with employers through representatives of their own choice. The ALRB investigates charges of unfair labor practices, holds representation elections, and adjudicates disputes over those elections. The board's five members are appointed by the governor and confirmed by the Senate. Board members serve five-year terms.

The *California Arts Council*, established in 1978, assists independent local groups in the development of arts programs and promotes the employment of artists and those skilled in crafts in the public and private sector. The council also provides for the exhibition of artworks in public buildings throughout California.

The council's 11 members, appointed by the governor and the legislature, focus on developing grant programs to support artists in various disciplines. Council members serve four-year staggered terms without salary.

The *California Horse Racing Board* supervises all horse race meetings in the state where parimutuel wagering is allowed. It licenses all horse racing participants, contracts with stewards to officiate at all races, enforces regulations under which racing is conducted, and collects the state's horse racing revenues. The seven-member board is appointed by the governor to four-year terms.

The *California Lottery Commission* was authorized in the initiative establishing a state lottery approved by the voters in 1984. The five commissioners, appointed by the governor, set policy for the California Lottery by interpreting the lottery act. The operation of the lottery is administered by the director, who is also appointed by the governor.

The *California Public Utilities Commission* regulates the safety, standards of service, and rates of privately-owned and operated natural gas, electric, telephone, water, sewer, steam and pipeline utilities as well as truck, bus, railroad, light rail, ferry and other transportation companies in California.

The CPUC does not regulate city-owned or municipal or district-owned utilities, or mutual water companies. The constitution gives the CPUC quasi-legislative and quasi-judicial authority.

Five commissioners are appointed by the governor, with the approval of the Senate, for a term of six years. They make all final policy, procedural and other decisions. Their terms are staggered to assure that the commission always has the benefit of experienced members.

The *California State World Trade Commission* offers financial and marketing assistance to California small and medium-sized companies once they have developed a product and are ready to export it. The Commissions Export Finance Office provides loan guarantees for some export transactions. The commission's office of Export Development offers a comprehensive export development program. The commission, created in 1983, is guided by a 15-member board.

The *Commission for Economic Development* provides guidance on statewide economic development by identifying and assessing regional and local economic development problems and making recommendations for solving them. It provides a forum for dialogue between state government and the private sector and undertakes special studies at the request of the governor or the legislature. The commission has 17 members, including six members of the legislature, and is chaired by the lieutenant governor.

The *Commission on California State Government Organization and Economy,* better known as the Little Hoover Commission, is a bipartisan body which makes independent studies and recommendations to the governor and the legislature on ways to promote economy and efficiency in state government. The commission consists of 13 members: nine public members appointed by the governor and the legislature, two senators, and two assembly members.

The *Commission on the Status of Women* is a 17-member body that works to eliminate inequities in laws, practices, and conditions which particularly affect women. The commission reviews all legislation affecting women's issues, maintains an information center on current needs of women, and consults with organizations working to assist women.

The *Council on California's Competitiveness*, created in December 1991, has the responsibility of finding ways to help the state compete economically and create new jobs. The 17-member volunteer council addresses the issues of worker education, workers' compensation, tort liability and liability reform, state and local regulatory burden, tax structure, and foreign market access.

PROVIDING PUBLIC SCHOOLS

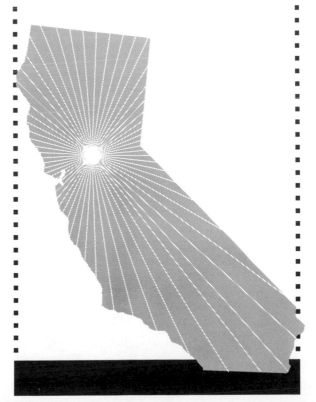

14

THE EDUCATIONAL SYSTEM

Under the U.S. Constitution public education is a responsibility reserved to the states. Thus the nation has 50 state school systems differing widely in organization, financial resources, and effectiveness. In recent years California schools have stressed higher standards in basic academic subjects, a longer school day and year, and the recruitment and retention of superior teachers.

The public school system in California is the largest in the nation serving more than 5.1 million students in 1991-92. The compulsory school age is six to 16 years, and continuation education is compulsory until 18 or the completion of high school. Adult education programs, community colleges, the California State University, and the University of California offer opportunities for lifelong learning.

ELEMENTARY AND SECONDARY EDUCATION

California's public schools are the shared responsibility of state government and local school districts. The legislature requires the formation of local districts and grants certain powers to them. State laws require specific programs and courses of study and provide a growing percentage of school funding.

DEPARTMENT OF EDUCATION

The *superintendent of public instruction*, a constitutional officer elected without party affiliation to a four-year term, directs the Department of Education. The superintendent is the chief administrative officer of the public school system, and provides leadership in developing and implementing strategies to improve education in the state's public schools. The superintendent also serves as an ex-officio member of the governing boards of the University of California and the California State University.

The *state Board of Education* is the policy-making body for public elementary and secondary education. The board has responsibility for studying the educational needs of California and for adopting plans for the improvement of the school system from kindergarten through grade 12. While the board develops general policy, both the legislature and local school boards exert strong influence on the direction of educational policies and programs.

The board consists of ten members who are appointed by the governor for four-year terms and serve without salary. In addition, one student is appointed for a one-year term. The superintendent of public instruction serves as secretary and executive officer of the board.

The Department of Education develops and administers programs which are implemented by local school districts. Although many of these programs are incorporated into regular classroom instruction, others require special facilities and considerable supervision at the state level.

The department administers a variety of child care and development programs which provide a full or part-day comprehensive program for young children. These subsidized services are provided to low-income families while parents are going to school, participating in training programs, working or seeking employment.

The department also takes an active role in the field of special education. Because students with exceptional needs require different and specialized educational services, various learning experiences are provided without charge to handicapped students from ages three to 21. Students are placed on the basis of their individual instructional needs rather than on the nature of their handicaps. Supplements such as tutoring can be added to a pupil's regular program, or alternative programs such as full-time special classes or sheltered workshops can be prescribed. Whenever possible, students are integrated into regular classrooms. Under the Master Plan for Special Education, these services are provided by regional organizations, which adopt special education plans for all school districts within the region.

The Department of Education operates three residential schools and three diagnostic centers to serve the unique needs of special education students. The California School for the Blind in Fremont, and the California Schools for the Deaf in Riverside and Fremont provide comprehensive education and related services to the state's visually and aurally impaired students. The Diagnostic Centers, located in San Francisco, Fresno, and Los Angeles, provide assessment services for special education students throughout California. Additionally, the Centers provide support services to local education agencies, service organizations, and other education-related groups.

COUNTY OFFICES OF EDUCATION

County offices of education operate their own educational programs such as schools, juvenile halls, regional occupation centers providing job-related training, special education classes and schools for handicapped students, and environmental education schools. In addition, county offices provide administrative and supportive services to small local school districts.

The county superintendent of schools is the chief executive officer of a county office of education. The superintendent also serves as secretary of the county board of education, which is the policy-making body for the county office and serves as the governing board for all educational programs operated at the county level. The constitution provides for a superintendent of schools in each county; voters determine whether the superintendent is elected or appointed.

LOCAL SCHOOL DISTRICTS

School districts are organized to provide education in several different grade spans, although the Legislature has encouraged the formation of unified school districts, those serving kindergarten through grade 12 (K-12). Other typical districts are elementary districts with grades K-6 or K-8 and high school districts. In 1992, there were 1,009 school districts in California.

All districts provide for an elected governing board of three to seven members serving four-year terms. Vacancies are filled by special election, although a city charter may provide for appointment. Many school board members serve without pay but are reimbursed for expenses. Some districts have chosen to set salaries for board members.

The school board sets local educational policies within the limits of state law and determines the curriculum. It adopts a budget and authorizes operating and capital expenditures. The school board is responsible for meeting federal desegregation guidelines in its schools by reassigning students, establishing management schools, or other means. In 1989-90, 13 school districts in California were implementing court-ordered desegregation plans.

The school board selects the superintendent, a professional educator who serves as administrative officer of the school district. The superintendent of a city or unified school district is hired on a four-year contract; other districts may contract for one to four years.

Teachers. California's public schools employ more than 221,000 teachers. Licenses or credentials are required for teachers in grades K-12 and are issued by the Commission on Teacher Credentialing, an independent body. In addition to this primary responsibility, the commission approves teacher preparation programs in colleges and universities and has the authority to revoke credentials.

Since 1983, prospective teachers have been required to pass minimum competency tests in verbal, mathematics, and writing skills. Minimum salaries for teachers are set by state law. State law also sets a maximum ratio of administrators to teachers. Districts are penalized for violations of these provisions by loss of state funds.

Teachers are given tenure (permanent status) after two consecutive years of satisfactory service and selection for employment for the third year. A probationary teacher may be dismissed only for cause. A permanent teacher may be dismissed only on specific charges of incompetency, immoral or unprofessional conduct, or conviction of a felony or crime involving moral turpitude. After being notified of charges a teacher may request a hearing before the Commission on Professional Competence. If dismissal is ordered, the teacher may appeal to the courts.

The Mentor Teacher program, begun in 1983, is designed to acknowledge and reward outstanding classroom teachers. Nominees are chosen by panels composed mostly of teachers; the school board makes the final selections. Mentor teachers receive an additional annual stipend and in return support other staff members, especially new teachers, and help develop curriculum.

Testing. Students are given minimum competency tests in reading writing, and mathematics once in grades four through six, once in grades seven through nine, and twice in grades ten through twelve. Students must pass both district established proficiency levels and specific course requirements. Counseling and remedial instruction must be provided for those who fail. No student is permitted to graduate from high school who has not met locally determined levels of competency.

In addition to competency testing, all students in grades four, five, eight, and ten will be assessed as part of the new California student assessment system. In addition, six Golden State Examinations—in first-year algebra, geometry, U.S. history, economics, chemistry, and biology—will be available on a voluntary basis to students enrolled in these subjects.

The purpose of the California student assessment system is to provide information to students, schools, districts, and the public about their educational progress in relation to performance expectations. With this information, students will know how they can achieve at higher levels and teachers can provide assistance most helpful to students.

School Calendar. Schools must be in session at least 175 days a year. Districts that operate at least 180 days per year receive additional incentive funding from the state, as do districts that have increased the length of the school day. Beginning in 1985, the average school day to qualify for incentive funding was increased in stages to at least 360 minutes in class for high schools, 300 minutes for fourth through eighth grades, 280 minutes for first though third grades, and 200 minutes for kindergarten.

Most schools operate on a September through early June calendar, but some operate year round with students attending on a rotating basis. (Year-round schools may have as few as 163 instructional days for each track, so long as they lengthen their days to provide at least the same total annual minutes of instruction as a regular 180-day-year school.) Two separate, free summer school programs are directed toward instruction in the core curriculum for all grades and basic skills remediation for low-achieving pupils in grades seven through twelve.

Curriculum. The suggested curriculum for California's schools (K-12) is described in curriculum frameworks. Curriculum frameworks describe current research in a subject area, the current state of curriculum and instruction, textbooks, testing, and teacher training. The frameworks represent a consensus among teachers, curriculum specialists, administrators, and faculty from colleges and universities on education in each subject area. Frameworks are based on Education Code Section 510002 which states that there is a need for a common state curriculum, but because of economic, geographic, physical, political, and social diversity in California, there is also a need to develop educational programs at the local level, with the guidance of competent and experienced educators and citizens. The frameworks are intended to be guidelines for districts to use in developing educational programs to meet the needs and interests of their students. Curriculum frameworks are available in the following subjects: English-language arts, history-social science, foreign language, visual and performing arts, science, mathematics, health, and one is currently being developed in physical education.

The curriculum frameworks also provide the basis for the development of criteria for selecting instructional materials, kindergarten through grade twelve. The state constitution requires the state Board of Education to review and adopt textbooks, to be furnished without cost, for use in grades one through eight throughout the state. The state also subsidizes the cost of textbooks used in high schools but does not adopt high school texts. As with frameworks, the state adopted instructional materials provide guidelines to districts in choosing instructional materials. The law states that because of the great diversity within California, the choice of textbooks and instructional materials shall be made locally. The state encourages districts to involve teachers and the local community in the selection process. Individual districts are free to use their own funds to supplement the state-supplied materials.

Educational programs. Although funding and policy guidelines come from the state and federal governments, it is the local school districts that implement and administer educational programs. Some programs are designed to meet the special needs of particular students; others attempt to improve the educational environment for all students. The 50 specific programs available in California schools include the following:

- The Economic Impact Aid program provides state funds to schools which are located in low income areas or have large numbers of students with poor academic skills. A federal program, ECIA Chapter I, directs funds into the same target areas. These programs emphasize instruction in the basic skills of reading, language, and mathematics and include auxiliary services such as counseling and health services.

- The School Improvement program provides additional funds directly to most local elementary and middle schools and some high schools. Decisions on how to spend the money, such as providing release time for curriculum, planning and professional development, or purchasing extra materials, are made at the individual school level by a school site council made up of school staff and parents.
- The Miller-Unruh reading program contributes toward the salaries of specialists who provide supplementary instruction for elementary school children with reading disabilities. Priority is given to the youngest children, those in grades K through three.
- Federal and state bilingual education programs are designed to accommodate the special needs of children with no English skills.
- The Gifted and Talented program provides differentiated and learning opportunities within the core curriculum for children with identified high intellectual, creative, or leadership abilities. Each district's program is determined locally, within state guidelines.
- Federal and state migrant education programs provide services to children of migrant workers, including supplementing the regular school program with preschool, extended day programs, and summer school.

Vocational Education. Career-vocational education programs provide high school students and adults with instruction and support services necessary for success and productivity at home and work. These programs also offer postsecondary education and training institutions to the broader community. Programs primarily occur as part of regular high schools, and regional occupational centers and programs; some are located in continuation and adult schools. The emphasis in career-vocational education is to integrate academics, applied academics, general employability, and occupational education developed in partnership with business and industry.

Adult education. Adult education programs meet a wide range of educational needs. Emphasis is given to improving basic educational skills for adults needing remediation and for those who are not proficient in English. Federal funds are available for basic skills instruction for students functioning below the the eighth grade level. An individual who does not have a high school diploma may earn one through adult education courses.

Other programs are designed to meet the special needs of older persons and persons with disabilities and to improve the students' vocational and parenting skills. Personal enrichment and recreation classes are offered on a fee basis.

SCHOOL FINANCE

Sources of funding. The amount of funding available to any California school district is primarily determined by the state. Since 1972, the basic financing of school districts has been controlled through a system of "revenue limits" governed by state law and annually adjusted through state budget policy. In 1991-92, local property taxes provided $5.3 billion (20.4 percent) of school money, but every district's total of property tax and state general aid is set by the state legislature. The state provided $16.1 billion (61.5 percent) for schools in 1991-92, as well as $485 million (1.9 percent) from the state lottery. Another $2.2 billion (8.6 percent) derives from local sources including parcel taxes, the sale and lease of property, and developer fees; and $2 billion (7.4 percent) federal funding completes the school funding picture.

Federal assistance to K-12 schools comes mostly in the form of "categorical" grants of aid for special programs. The federal government also provides a kind of general aid to some districts where federal employees live and work. This form of assistance, known as "impact aid" has been declining in recent years as federal military base closures have reduced the number of federal dependents. Thirty-four percent of the California State Lottery's total sales are allocated for public education. Lottery money is shared proportionately by all levels of public education, from kindergarten through the college and university level. School districts and governing bodies decide how to spend the money, which by law may be used for any instructional purpose except research or the purchase or construction of facilities.

Another initiative, Proposition 98 **(see Figure 14.1 — About Proposition 98)** from the November 1988 ballot, established a Constitutional guarantee designed to ensure that annual state funding for K-14 education would keep up with state revenue growth, enrollment growth, and cost-of-living increases. In addition to setting a minimum level for total state funding, Proposition 98 entitled school districts and community colleges to a share of any future state revenues that exceed the states' expenditure limit ("Gann spending limit") and required public schools to issue annual "report cards" to the public providing an array of basic data. It is considered unlikely that the State will ever collect revenues in excess of the limit, so these other aspects of Proposition 98 are not well known.

Methods of funding. Public schools traditionally have been financed on a shared basis by the local school districts and the state, with the local districts drawing upon the local property tax and the state drawing upon the General Fund. The larger share used to come from local property taxes. Under this system the amount of money available for public education depended upon two factors: the tax rate of the school district and the assessed value of the taxable property in the district. Thus, a low tax rate in one district might produce a high level of support per pupil, while in another district even a high tax rate would produce only a low level of support because the assessed value of property was much less.

The resulting disparity in dollar expenditures per pupil among districts with similar tax rates prompted a suit against the state. In

ABOUT PROPOSITION 98

This constitutional amendment, narrowly approved by the voters in November 1988, took effect in the 1989-90 school year. As amended by Proposition 111 in 1990, Prop. 98 has four provisions:

• Minimum funding guarantee for K-12 schools and community colleges based on the same share of the General Fund as the base year 1986-87 or the prior year's funding from state and property taxes adjusted for inflation (growth in per capita personal income) and enrollment increases in high revenue growth years. In low revenue growth years, (when General Fund tax revenues grow more slowly than per capita personal income) inflation is defined as growth in per capita General Fund revenues plus one-half percent.

• Payment to K-14 education of 50 percent of the excess when state tax revenues exceed the Gann spending limit; the remaining 50 percent is rebated to the taxpayers.

• Annual School Accountability Report Cards (SARCs) listing at least 13 specific items.

• A "prudent" state budget reserve.

Proposition 98 may be suspended for one year by a two-thirds vote of the legislature and the governor's signature.

Source: Office of the Secretary of State, EdSource

Figure 14.1

Serrano v. Priest (1971), the California Supreme Court ruled that it is a violation of the equal protection clause of the California constitution to allow the amount of educational spending per pupil to be determined by the taxable property wealth of the district where the student lives. The legislature was ordered to restructure school finance methods to reduce the disparities caused by property tax wealth to less than $100 per pupil. In 1974-75, slightly more than 50 percent of school children lived in school districts that met that requirement. By 1990-91, this figure had risen to 96 percent, but the $100 had also been increased to $290 for inflation.

The basic mechanism for distributing public funds to schools is average daily attendance (ADA), defined as the average number of students either in school or validly absent each day. In 1991-92, spending for each K-12 student in California averaged approximately $4,672.

Under California's present system of financing schools, state funds are allocated to school districts through a "revenue limit" system. Each district's revenue limit represents the level of funding per ADA to which the district is entitled, with revenue limits approximately the same throughout the state for districts of similar size and type. This designated level of funding is financed through a combination of local property tax and state aid. In school districts where the amount of property tax received is not sufficient to reach the revenue limit, the state makes up the difference. The state guarantees each school district an amount of general purpose funds equal to its revenue limit times its ADA.

In addition the constitution requires that each district receive "basic aid" of $120 per ADA or $2,400, whichever is greater. In most school districts, where the amount of local property tax is less than the revenue limit, the state makes up the difference and counts this amount against the constitutionally required basic aid. In the handful of school districts where the property tax wealth exceeds the revenue limit, the basic aid provides additional funding.

In addition to these unrestricted funds, school districts receive funds which can be used only for special purposes, such as those for the School Improvement Program or Miller-Unruh reading specialists. About one-quarter of a school district's funding is in the form of such categorical aid.

POSTSECONDARY EDUCATION

Education beyond the high school level includes specialized vocational and technical training, degree programs in the sciences and liberal arts, and postgraduate professional schools. California's public postsecondary education system is the largest in the nation, serving over 1.7 million students annually at 137 campuses throughout the state.

The *California Postsecondary Education Commission* was created in 1973 to provide coordination and planning for higher education. It makes recommendations to the governor and legislature on budgets, admissions policies, proposed academic and occupational programs, and student fee and aid levels.

The commission is composed of 17 members, nine of whom represent the general public and are appointed by the governor and legislative leaders. Six members represent public and private postsecondary institutions and organizations and two members represent students and are appointed by the governor.

The *Student Aid Commission* administers several state and federal financial aid programs, including loans, grants, and college work-study. Any student attending an accredited public or private college or university in California is eligible for such assistance. The most common form of assistance is the loan, awarded on the basis of financial need, and the largest program is the federal Guaranteed Student Loan Program.

The *Master Plan for Higher Education* was created in 1960 at a time when increasing enrollments, rising costs, and competition for funds, prestige, and new facilities prompted the need for coordination among the various higher education institutions. The original Master Plan created separate statewide governing boards for what became the California Community Colleges and the California State University (the University of California was already established in the Constitution and governed by the Regents). It also led to the creation of a statewide higher education coordinating council, now known as the California Postsecondary Education Commission. The Master Plan provided for the differentiation of function among the three segments of higher education. The specific roles of each segment are discussed in the following descriptions.

In addition to differentiation by function, the Master Plan also differentiated the pool of students from which each segment was to draw: UC from the top one-eighth of the high school graduating class; CSU from the top one-third; and the community colleges are to accept every Californian with a high school diploma or age 18 or above. The Master Plan has undergone two exhaustive reviews—in the mid-1970's and in the late 1980's. In particular, the most recent review emphasized the importance of being able to accommodate growing numbers of students from ethnically and economically diverse backgrounds.

COMMUNITY COLLEGES

More than 1.5 million students attend California's community colleges. Total enrollment is twice that of CSU and UC combined and represents one-fourth of community college enrollment nationwide. The student body is diverse in age, skill level, and academic goals; many attend part-time. Anyone over 18 years of age is eligible for admission; a high school diploma is not a prerequisite.

The community college system offers several different programs, including a two-year curriculum leading to an associate degree in arts or sciences. A student with a good academic record may transfer to a four-year institution to earn a higher degree. Vocational and technical education programs have become an increasingly important part of the community college curriculum; numerous occupational certificates and credentials may be earned. Community colleges also provide instruction in citizenship and remedial skills. In addition, non-credit, community service classes such as landscaping are offered on a self-supporting fee basis.

California has 71 community college districts which operate 107 campuses throughout the state. Unlike the University of California and California State University systems, community college districts are administered by their own locally elected boards of trustees as well as a statewide board of governors. The local boards approve curriculum and allocate funds to the programs and campuses within their jurisdiction. They also select the president of each college.

A statewide board of governors, composed of 16 members who are appointed by the governor, provides board policy guidance to the system. The board adopts regulations for all community colleges, allocates state and federal funds to districts, and reviews academic programs and construction of facilities. The board appoints a chancellor, who is the chief administrative officer of the system.

CALIFORNIA STATE UNIVERSITY

The individual California State Colleges were brought together as a system in 1960. In 1972, the system became the California State University and Colleges, and 14 of the 19 campuses became universities. Now all of the campuses are universities, including the addition of the twentieth campus in San Marcos.

Admission is open to all eligible students from the top third of high school graduates. Admission standards may be waived in a limited number of cases to encourage minority enrollment.

The California State University system is oriented to undergraduate education, and offers a broad range of liberal arts, sciences, and occupational undergraduate degrees. The Master Plan for Higher Education assigns primary responsibility for teacher education to the CSU system; each campus offers credential programs for elementary, high school, and special education teachers. CSU also provides graduate instruction at the masters degree level; it awards some doctoral degrees jointly with the University of California.

Responsibility for CSU is vested in the board of trustees. The board consists of 18 members appointed by the governor to eight-year terms and five ex-officio members—the governor, lieutenant governor, speaker of the Assembly, superintendent of public instruction, and chancellor of CSU. The board of trustees appoints the chancellor, who is the chief executive officer of the system, and the presidents, who are

UNIVERSITY OF CALIFORNIA CAMPUSES

Berkeley	Irvine	Riverside	Santa Barbara
Davis	Los Angeles	San Diego	Santa Cruz
		San Francisco	

CALIFORNIA STATE UNIVERSITY CAMPUSES

Bakersfield	Hayward	Pomona*	San Jose
Chico	Humboldt	Sacramento	San Luis Obispo*
Dominguez Hills	Los Angeles	San Bernardino	San Marcos
Fresno	Long Beach	San Diego	Sonoma
Fullerton	Northridge	San Francisco	Stanislaus

Polytechnic Universities

Figure 14.2

the chief executive officers of the respective campuses.

UNIVERSITY OF CALIFORNIA

The University of California has grown from one campus of 38 students in 1868 to one of the world's largest centers for higher education. The university has eight general campuses as well as one health sciences campus in San Francisco and numerous research facilities. Hastings College of the Law, located in San Francisco, is affiliated with the University, although it remains administratively separate.

Admission to the University of California is open to high school students graduating in the top eighth of their class. Nearly all of those enrolled in the university are full-time students.

The university has three roles: instruction, research, and public service. It provides undergraduate and graduate instruction in the liberal arts, sciences, and the professions and awards doctoral degrees. It has exclusive jurisdiction in public higher education over instruction in the professions of law, medicine, dentistry, and veterinary medicine.

The University of California is the primary state-supported agency for research. The Lick Observatory, the Scripps Institute of Oceanography, and the Air Pollution Research Center are some of the many research facilities. Under contract with the U.S. Department of Energy, the university conducts research programs in nuclear energy at the Lawrence Laboratories in Livermore and Berkeley and the Los Alamos Scientific Laboratory in New Mexico.

The university maintains medical schools and teaching hospitals at five campuses. In addition to their role in clinical instruction, these centers serve as community resources for highly specialized medical care. Other public services of the university include agricultural information services and a broad program of continuing education for adults in the arts, business, and professions.

To govern the university, the constitution grants authority to a 26-member Board of Regents—a board that has substantial freedom from legislative or executive control. Seven members of the board are ex-officio: the governor, lieutenant governor, speaker of the Assembly, superintendent of public instruction, president and vice president of the alumni association, and president of the university. Eighteen additional members are appointed by the governor with approval of the Senate, for twelve-year terms. A university student selected by the Regents from a pool of candidates nominated by the University of California Student Association, is appointed to a one-year term by the board. In addition, two faculty representatives (the Chair and Vice Chair of the Academic Council) serve as non-voting members of the board. In selecting Regents, the governor must consult a constitutionally established advisory committee. The constitution requires that the regents "shall be able persons broadly reflective of the economic, cultural, and social diversity of the state, including ethnic minorities and women."

The Regents appoint the president of the university, who is its executive head. With the advice of the president, they appoint chancellors and deans, who administer the affairs of the individual campuses.

OTHER POSTSECONDARY INSTITUTIONS

California has three other publicly supported postsecondary institutions: the Otis Art Institute of Los Angeles, locally financed; the U.S. Naval Postgraduate School at Monterey, federally financed; and the California Maritime Academy in Vallejo, state financed. The Maritime Academy is one of only six institutions in the United States that provide a program for men and women who seek to become licensed officers in the Merchant Marine. It is governed by an independent board of governors composed of seven members appointed by the governor for four-year terms.

More than 1,600-private vocational and technical schools serve the specialized educational needs of thousands of Californians. They offer courses in a wide variety of fields such as business, barbering, and cosmetology. The Council for Private Postsecondary and Vocational Education issues certifications of approval to these private schools.

FINANCING POSTSECONDARY EDUCATION

In 1991-92, a total of $15.9 billion in state General Funds was appropriated to higher education in California for current operations, compared to $17.7 billion for K-12 education. The state General Fund is the largest single source of income for postsecondary education. The federal government is another large contributor, providing funds primarily for research and student financial aid programs rather than for instructional expenses. The three systems of higher education, community colleges, California State University, and the University of California, vary in the sources of their funds and the autonomy with which they are spent.

Education in public postsecondary schools traditionally has been tuition free to California residents. However, student fees are charged for services not directly related to instruction, such as health services and recreation. In 1991-92, the annual student fee for a full-time undergraduate student was $120 at community colleges, $1,088 at CSU and $2,486 at UC. Financial assistance is available to eligible students.

In terms of funding, community colleges have more in common with K-12 schools than with other postsecondary institutions. Community colleges receive about three-fourths of their funding from the state General Fund, the same percentage as do K-12 schools. Funds are allocated on the basis of full-time equivalent (FTE) students. The community college is the only segment of higher education receiving local support, as property tax revenues provide their second largest source of income. Through the state budget process, the governor and the legislature set some spending policies and determine the total state contribution to the community college system. The system's Board of Governors and the chancellor allocate funds to the 70 individual districts; the locally elected boards and the campus presidents decide how funds will be spent within individual districts and colleges.

The California State University system is supported primarily by the state General Fund. The governor and the legislature exercise considerable control over financial decisions by the use of line-item budget appropriations. Funds are allocated to individual campuses by the statewide board of trustees and the chancellor.

The University of California system is supported primarily by a combination of state General Funds, federal funds, gifts, grants, endowments and student fees. Unlike the governing bodies of the community college and CSU systems, the Board of Regents and the officers of the individual UC campuses have substantial autonomy in deciding how to spend their funds. Over half of the total federal funds spent for higher education in California go to the university's research laboratories which are funded by the U.S. Department of Energy.

Capital improvements traditionally have been financed from direct appropriations from the state General Fund and the Capital Outlay Fund for Public Higher Education (COFPHE or "coffee" fund), which receives its revenue from the state's tidelands oil operations. However, since 1986 capital improvements have been funded primarily from General Obligation bonds, the High Technology Education Revenue Bond Program and other revenue bonds.

Capital outlay funds are used for new construction, major repair or remodeling projects, or unusually large equipment purchases. The annual state budget lists each major capital expenditure at each campus individually. Minor capital improvements (those costing less than $200,000 per project) are authorized in a lump sum by the legislature and are allocated to individual projects and campuses by the administrative boards of the colleges and universities. Such improvements are designed to alter existing facilities to meet changing program needs, make needed repairs, provide handicapped access, or meet fire and safety requirements, such as the removal of hazardous asbestos. Local governments have no role in funding capital improvements for the UC and CSU systems.

STATE LIBRARY

Located in Sacramento, the state library provides research and reference materials for officials, legislators, and other state employees. The library maintains several specialized collections, including law, government publications, and California history. The public may use the library's collections and may borrow materials through their local libraries on inter-library loan.

The library provides special services to visually-impaired and physically challenged individuals. Volumes in braille, phonograph records, and audio cassettes are circulated to eligible individuals through the mail.

While local libraries are locally administered, the state library makes consulting, reference, and inter-library loan services available to them. It also administers several grant programs to enable local libraries to extend their services.

The Sutro Library in San Francisco, which houses rare books and reference materials on genealogy, Mexican and English history, is also part of the state library.

WORKING WITH OTHER LEVELS

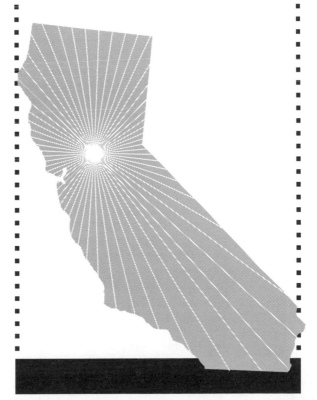

15

COUNTY GOVERNMENT

In its beginning decades, California state government performed relatively few functions, assigning to counties the responsibility for governmental services which the legislature designated as necessary. Thus, counties were the governmental units which built roads, maintained jails, cared for the poor and kept records on property and statistics on people. Today, counties perform greatly expanded services. Some counties provide services not only mandated by the state, but assumed under laws giving counties the option of providing additional services appropriate to local circumstances.

Counties are geographical and political subdivisions of the state and thus serve as important administrative units for state and often federal laws, programs and services. In fact, more than 55 percent of county revenues come from these two sources. As agents of state government, with the same functions delegated to all of them, counties are subject to extensive state administrative supervision and regulation. At the same time, counties still have some local autonomy. County government is in the hands of elected officials responsible to local citizens. These officials deal with needs, wants and resources which differ greatly from county to county.

STRUCTURE OF COUNTY GOVERNMENT

California's 58 counties vary greatly in size, geography and population. San Bernardino County, the largest in area, is 46 times as large as Santa Cruz County, the smallest except for the combined city-county of San Francisco. The population of Los Angeles County is nearly nine million, while fewer than 1,200 people live in the mountains and forests of Alpine County. How are these differences accommodated? While the legislature may pass special laws for particular counties, state law also grants broad discretionary powers. Counties may adapt their internal structure, operations and programs to local conditions.

COUNTY FORMATION

The years have seen changes in the boundaries of counties. While they are stable, they are not immutable. During the state's first 60 years, the original 27 counties of 1850 became 58. Although legally possible, forming a new county is politically difficult.

In 1974, the legislature eased the procedural requirements but every one of the eight attempts has failed. The state constitution requires that formation of a new county must be approved by a majority of those voting on the question in each county concerned.

GENERAL LAW AND CHARTER COUNTIES

The state constitution provides for three classes of county government: general law, charter, or consolidated city and county (which must be a charter unit). There are 12 charter counties: Alameda, Butte, Fresno, Los Angeles, Placer, Sacramento, San Bernardino, San Diego, San Francisco (the only city-county), San Mateo, Santa Clara and Tehama. The procedures for adoption or amendment of county charters are the same as for city charters.

The main difference between general law and charter counties lies in the way they can organize and select their county governing bodies and officers. Every county is required to elect a governing body — a board of supervisors. General law counties elect supervisors by district, while charter counties have the option of electing them at large or by district. Except for the constitutional requirement that every county elect a sheriff, district attorney and an assessor, charter counties have considerable freedom when drafting their charters to determine what other officers they will have, their powers and duties, and whether they will be elected or appointed. Although general law counties have been granted some flexibility, they do not have the latitude of charter counties regarding officers. General law counties are regulated by statutes which specify their principal officers, assign their duties and require that they be elected by the people. The law, however, permits boards of supervisors to consolidate these elective offices into any of 25 combinations and to appoint additional officers, but prohibits the supervisors from giving appointed officials the responsibilities assigned by law to elected officials.

FUNCTIONS OF COUNTY GOVERNMENT POLICY MAKING

California counties have five supervisors elected for four-year staggered terms on a nonpartisan ballot, except for the city-county of San Francisco, which has 11 supervisors and a mayor. If a supervisorial position becomes vacant between elections, it is filled by the governor in general law counties. Charter counties may make other provisions for filling vacancies. In all counties, supervisorial district boundaries must be adjusted after each federal census so that the population of all

CALIFORNIA'S 58 COUNTIES

Figure 15.1

districts is as nearly equal as possible.

The board of supervisors is the legislative and executive body of county government. The supervisors pass all ordinances governing the county and are responsible for seeing that functions delegated to the county are properly discharged. They adopt the budget, set employee salaries and make determinations in personnel matters when there is no independent personnel board or civil service system. They are in charge of public works, including the county road system, and serve in ex-officio capacity as the board of directors for special districts of various kinds. Supervisors also represent their counties on councils of government (COGs) and other regional bodies.

The board of supervisors has responsibility for overseeing a variety of services to county residents, including those in cities as well as those in unincorporated areas. Such countywide services include voter registration, health and welfare programs, court and law enforcement operations, jail facilities, the recording of official documents, including vital statistics and real property transactions, tax assessment and collection, and social services.

The supervisors are also responsible for providing some municipal-type services for residents of unincorporated areas. These include planning, zoning and land-use regulation, street maintenance, and in some cases sewage disposal, water, parks and recreational facilities and other municipal services. Policy decisions on the degree of service lie with the board of supervisors. Highly urbanized unincorporated areas may have the same service needs as conventional cities. These needs are frequently met by formation of special districts.

The board of supervisors also has some quasi-judicial functions. For example, in many counties supervisors serve as the tax assessment appeals board and as the planning and land-use appeal body.

ADMINISTRATION

A *chief administrative officer* is appointed by the board of supervisors in most of the counties in the state. This officer is responsible for implementing board decisions, preparing the county budget, carrying out studies to provide the supervisors with information needed in making decisions and generally coordinating county administration. Although the county officer is often called "county manager" or "county executive," there is a legal distinction. Only charter counties may establish the position of county manager or executive, and in these cases the officer has more authority than a chief administrative officer who is essentially the agent of the board of supervisors.

Historically, the *county clerk* serves as the registrar of voters, ex-officio clerk of the board of supervisors, ex-officio clerk of the Superior Court and performs a variety of other functions such as issuing marriage licenses, processing passport applications and filing fictitious business names. In some counties, all of these functions have been retained by a single county officer; in others, the functions have been split into two or more offices.

The *county recorder* keeps records of births, deaths, marriages, all instruments recording real property and other documents required by law. In some counties, this office is combined with that of the county clerk.

A *county counsel* may be appointed by the supervisors to serve as chief legal adviser on civil matters for the county. The counsel may discharge the civil duties of the district attorney, advise county officials on their responsibilities and serve as attorney for them in their official capacity.

By charter or by ordinance approved by the electorate, a county may adopt a civil service system administered by an independent *personnel board*. Most counties have some form of civil service covering most of the non-elected personnel. Some counties arrange with the state Personnel Board for merit system assistance. All counties provide some kind of retirement plan for officials and employees, either by contract with the Public Employees' Retirement System or through an independent retirement system.

The *public administrator* is responsible for the administration of the estates of persons deceased without apparent heirs. On appointment by the court, the public administrator serves as guardian for people—often minors or the elderly—who are not competent to manage their affairs and lack private assistance.

FINANCE

The chief financial officer of the county is the *auditor* or director of finance. The auditor monitors the financial records of all county departments, reports on the state of the county's finances and authorizes expenditures by warrants.

The *treasurer* is custodian of the county's money, pays county obligations on warrant from the auditor and assists in the collection of taxes.

The *assessor* appraises property in the county which is subject to taxation.

The *tax collector* collects all county taxes and deposits them with the treasurer.

COUNTY FINANCE

Total revenues received and collected by county government can be classified into five distinct categories. These categories, ranked from highest to lowest in terms of revenue are: state government, 31 percent; property taxes, 21 percent; federal government, 17 percent; enterprise receipts, 13 percent; and, charges for current services, eight percent. The balance is comprised of a variety of revenue sources.

PLANNING

A planning agency is mandatory in all counties. Every county except

Kern County has a *planning commission* appointed by the supervisors. The planning commission prepares and maintains a general plan for physical development of the county and reviews development plans for environmental impact. The commission is advisory to the supervisors, who approve and implement recommendations and hear appeals in disputes between citizens and the commission. State law allows the supervisors to appoint "area planning commissions" to plan and regulate land use within distinct communities.

A *local agency formation commission* is also mandatory, although it is not a county body but an independent commission consisting of representatives from the county, cities and the general public. In some counties, special districts also sit on LAFCO. Proposals for boundary changes such as municipal incorporation and annexation and formation or dissolution of independent special districts require LAFCO approval. LAFCOs must also adapt long-range service plans called "spheres of influence" for each city and special district in their county.

LAW ENFORCEMENT

The *sheriff* is the chief law enforcement officer in all unincorporated territory. The sheriff apprehends law violators and may be in charge of the jail and other custodial facilities. Other duties include implementing programs to prevent crime, reduce delinquency and rehabilitate criminals.

The *district attorney* is the public prosecutor and in counties without a county counsel performs the counsel's duties as well. The district attorney prosecutes those accused of crimes and presents evidence of crime to the grand jury.

A *public defender* is appointed or contracted for in most counties to defend people who are charged with offenses but are unable to pay for attorney services. The defender may bring civil cases on behalf of indigents for claims not over $100 or defend them in civil suits if no other legal aid is available.

The *coroner* investigates causes of deaths occurring without medical attention under violent or unusual circumstances. When the cause of death is uncertain, a coroner's jury may be called to see if further action is warranted.

The *chief probation officer* is responsible for monitoring persons placed on probation by the courts. In addition, the probation department may have the responsibility of administering one or more alternative sentencing programs, such as home detention.

Every county has a Superior Court which consists of a specified number of judges as prescribed by the legislature. Municipalities with populations of 40,000 or more may have at least one municipal court. The number of municipal court judges per county is specified and prescribed by the legislature.

Counties that do not have population centers of the size warranting municipal court judges may have justice court judges. Justice court judges generally are found in the state's rural counties or in isolated areas in larger counties, such as the Santa Catalina Justice Court in Los Angeles County.

PUBLIC HEALTH

Pursuant to statutory mandate, counties provide medical services for medically indigent people. The system of indigent medical care varies from county to county and may involve county hospitals and clinics, contracts with private hospitals and clinics or a mixture of both public and private facilities. Some small counties contract with the state for provision of indigent medical care services in a system similar to Medi-Cal.

County public health departments provide an array of services for people of all ages, including emergency medical services, infectious disease control, immunizations, public health labs, drug and alcohol abuse prevention/intervention/treatment, tobacco education, child health screenings/treatment, dental services, home health services, family planning, perinatal services, special services for seniors, AIDS testing/counseling/education and vital statistics.

Environmental health, air pollution control and animal control are county responsibilities and may be included in the health department.

WELFARE

A major responsibility of the supervisors is the administration of welfare programs mandated by state and federal law. Before 1991, funding for these programs was largely provided by the state. In 1991, landmark legislation was passed by the legislature which shifted responsibility and funding for health, mental health and various social services programs from the state to counties. Each year, 40 percent of county expenditures is for public assistance. County welfare departments administer programs overseen by the state Health and Welfare Agency. These departments determine eligibility and benefits in the Aid to Families with Dependent Children, Medi-Cal and Food Stamp programs. County welfare departments also deliver social services to eligible persons in need of child care, family planning, health and homemaker services. They offer protective services to adults and children and are required to provide such services as foster care to children in danger of abuse and exploitation. Welfare departments also license care facilities and provide information and referral to anyone regardless of eligibility. In addition to mandated programs, some counties also provide emergency housing, legal assistance, sustenance programs and adoption services.

All counties are required to administer a general relief program that gives financial aid to needy individuals who are not served by established state and federal programs. Counties receive federal and state funds for support of many programs but each county must fund its own general relief program.

PUBLIC WORKS

Some counties employ a director of public works to assume responsibility for county buildings, roads, solid waste disposal and other physical facilities such as sewage treatment or flood control and drainage projects. A county surveyor conducts surveys where necessary for the overall public interest of having an adequate system of monuments, keeps survey records and supplies copies of maps required by the recorder's office. In some counties, the surveyor is also the county engineer. This office may also include building inspection.

LIBRARIES

The boards of supervisors establish and maintain free public libraries and appoint county librarians. Depending on the county, the county library may be administered as a special district or as a general fund department of county government. Funding for library operation comes from a combination of local property taxes and allocations from the state budget's public library fund. Although city libraries may exist as separate and independent local entities with their own administrations and budgets, in some counties the city and county libraries function as a consolidated system. Most public libraries belong to a statewide cooperative system.

OTHER OFFICES

Other county offices mandated for general law counties and common for charter counties include a fire marshal, a livestock inspector and a sealer of weights and measures. Among other officers the board of supervisors may appoint are an agricultural commissioner, a health officer, a public guardian and a public information officer.

INTERGOVERNMENTAL COOPERATION

Ninety percent of Californians live in 14 metropolitan areas and more than half live in the urban complexes of the Los Angeles Basin and San Francisco Bay. The concentrated population in such metropolitan areas has resulted in fragmented land-use planning, traffic congestion and environmental deterioration. In the absence of enforceable areawide planning, important decisions on land use and governmental policy can be made by many separate and unrelated governmental units. Intergovernmental cooperation (among cities, counties, schools, special districts, regional agencies and the state) is necessary for the balancing of interests, the efficient provision of services and agreement on long-term solutions in the best interests of the total region. Yet such cooperation can be difficult to achieve. California has developed a number of approaches to cooperation, including the Joint Exercise of Powers Act and legislation establishing regional organizations with considerable authority.

Shortly after California became a state, the city of San Francisco became a consolidated city-county. Since then, other counties have considered the step, but none has taken it. Sacramento voters rejected the idea in 1974 and 1990. In Los Angeles County, however, a number of so-called "contract cities" have been developed, which buy such urban services as water, waste removal and law enforcement from the county rather than provide them individually. This practice began in 1954 when the community of Lakewood, instead of annexing to Long Beach, incorporated and contracted with Los Angeles County to obtain needed services. Since then, most of the new cities in Los Angeles County have opted to adopt this "Lakewood Plan," also known as "functional consolidation." Other counties now also sell services to municipalities by contract.

COUNCILS OF GOVERNMENTS

A council of governments is a voluntary intergovernmental organization which functions as a regional forum for research, discussion, planning and recommendations. There are 25 such councils in California, comprised of representatives from member city and county governments. The councils range from bodies whose principal function is to prepare regional housing plans to such prominent organizations as the following:

ABAG, the Association of Bay Area Governments, has been in operation since 1961. All of the nine eligible counties and 96 of the 99 cities are members of the association. ABAG prepares regional plans and coordinates local governments' relations with the federal government. A major program developed by ABAG and funded by the federal Environmental Protection Agency promotes better air and water quality and solid waste management in the Bay area.

SCAG, the Southern California Association of Governments, created in 1965, has a membership of 139 of the 184 eligible cities and all six counties. The organization deals with areawide concerns in three policy areas: community, economic and human development; transportation and utilities; and energy and environment. Aided by technical advisory groups, SCAG committees make specific policy recommendations to local governments.

SACOG, the Sacramento Area Council of Governments, was created in 1980. SACOG covers four counties and part of a fifth, plus 15 cities. SACOG makes policy recommendations, gives technical planning assistance and provides funds and staff to small communities without planning agencies.

SANDAG, the San Diego Association of Governments, created in 1980, has a membership of all 18 cities and the County of San Diego. Besides planning for water, energy, transportation and housing, SANDAG acts as the Regional Transportation Commission, the Airport Land Use Commission and the Regional Growth Management Board.

MUNICIPAL ADVISORY COUNCILS

In recognition of the need by unincorporated communities for increased influence with their county boards of supervisors, municipal advisory councils have been organized in some counties under authorization of a 1971 legislative statute. Such a council is an advisory body of local citizens elected by the community or appointed by the board of supervisors with the purpose of representing the community to the board. Although a municipal advisory council is a governing body, it has no fiscal authority or administrative organization. Because it lacks authority to implement its position directly, it seeks to accomplish its goals through county government.

These councils face two ways: toward the county, offering the views of the community; and toward the community, supplying information about county proposals and a place where individuals can air opinions on community problems and perhaps receive help. The councils hold public meetings, survey community opinion and speak for the community to the board of supervisors. The most common subject of activity is land-use planning. The county often uses the group as a planning advisory council to draft or revise the community's portion of the county general plan.

16

CITY
GOVERNMENT

California cities are as diverse as the people who live in them. They range in size from Vernon, with a population of 152, to Los Angeles, with more than 3.5 million. Some, like Monterey, predate the formation of state government, tracing their development back to the days of the Spanish *presidios*. Other cities, like American Canyon and Lake Forest, are so new they are still forming their identity.

Regardless of size or age or corporate structure, city governments are responsible for providing services which directly affect the lives of their residents. Through fire and police protection, cities safeguard lives and property. They also construct and maintain streets, provide facilities for sewage, storm drainage, and waste disposal, and look after health, recreational and social needs. Most cities provide water; some provide public transportation systems; a few manage municipal utilities such as electricity or natural gas. City planning and zoning determine land use compatible with community economic, environmental, and cultural goals.

POWERS AND STRUCTURE OF CITY GOVERNMENT

To carry out the functions of local government, cities are granted powers by the state. City governments may legislate to protect the health, safety, and welfare of their people, provided that these regulations are not in conflict with state or federal law. They may generate revenue by levying taxes, by license and service fees, and by borrowing. They may employ needed personnel. They may condemn property for public use.

While their powers are derived from the state constitution and from laws enacted by the legislature, cities themselves are created only by the request and consent of the residents in a given area. Communities may incorporate as cities for many reasons–to control population growth and development, to gain local control of tax money, to provide services, to promote special interests, to solve specific problems, to provide a more responsive unit of government or to prevent annexation to adjoining cities.

GENERAL LAW AND CHARTER CITIES

All 468 California cities are municipal corporations. Their formation is provided for in the state constitution, and they fall into three categories: general law cities (more than four out of five cities in California), charter cities, and one consolidated city and county (San Francisco).

General law cities derive their powers from and organize their governments according to acts of the legislature. The fundamental law of these cities is found in the state Government Code, which enumerates their powers and specifies their structure.

Charter cities are formed when citizens specifically frame and adopt a charter or document to establish the organization and basic law of the city. The constitution guarantees to these charter cities a large measure of "home rule," granting to them, independent of the legislature, direct control over local affairs. There are 83 charter cities in California.

The basic difference between general law and charter cities is found in the degree of control which the state government may exercise over them. Charter cities have more freedom to innovate and to pass ordinances according to local need. General law cities nevertheless also have considerable choice in their form of municipal government, and fairly broad powers over local affairs. Because the legislature has tended to give general law cities the same control over internal matters that the constitution grants to charter cities, the original distinction between the two forms of city authority has been somewhat blurred.

DETERMINATION OF CITY BOUNDARIES

Incorporation may be initiated by resolution of a county board of supervisors or by citizen petition. The petition must be signed by at least 25 percent of the locally registered voters. A petition by landowners is possible, but rare. The petition is then submitted to the Local Agency Formation Commission (LAFCO), which reviews the proposed plan for incorporation (a feasibility study of boundaries, service provision, and potential revenues), conducts a hearing, and then, frequently after suggesting changes, approves or denies the proposal. If the petition is approved, the board of supervisors conducts a hearing. If a majority of the voters file written protests, the board must terminate the procedures. If there is no majority protest, the board must call an election. The incorporation must be approved by a majority of the voters living within the proposed city. If the vote is against incorporation, no proceedings to incorporate any of the same territory may be started for another two years.

After incorporation, a city may adopt a charter. Either an initiative petition or the governing body may call for an election to determine whether to draft or revise the charter and to elect a charter commission (the governing body may also serve in this capacity). When drafted, a charter must be approved by majority vote of the electorate. Amendment or repeal of a charter may be proposed either by the city council or by initiative, and adopted by majority vote of the electorate.

The question of disincorporation must be considered by a city council if petitioned by 20 percent of the city's voters. A majority of those voting in a special election determines the outcome. No city has disincorporated since 1972.

Annexation and consolidation procedures parallel those for incorporation. Any land area contiguous to a city in the same county may be annexed to the city if such annexation does not result in an island of unincorporated land completely surrounded by the city or in narrow strips of unincorporated land. (Because earlier law did not prohibit them, such islands currently exist in some cities.) In rare cases, LAFCO can make an exception.

Proponents of an annexation must have the approval of LAFCO and the governing body. In inhabited territory (with at least 12 voters), a petition signed by 25 percent of the qualified voters is filed with LAFCO. If LAFCO approves, then the city council calls a public hearing. If there is protest a special election is called. Annexation requires majority approval within the annexation area. Proposals for annexing uninhabited territory may be initiated by either the annexing city or the owners of the land. No election is held. If approved by LAFCO, the annexation occurs automatically, unless a protest is made by 50 percent or more of the owners of land and improvements in the area. A city cannot decline an annexation approved by LAFCO and not sufficiently protested, unless the annexation is very large relative to the city. Then an election is required.

Two or more cities may consolidate, but a city may not be annexed by, or consolidated with, another without majority approval of voters of both cities.

FUNCTIONS OF CITY GOVERNMENT

POLICY MAKING

City government is overseen in all cities by an elected governing body (city council) which establishes municipal policy and enacts and implements local ordinances. Council members may be elected at large or by district, or in charter cities may be nominated and elected in any manner stated in the charter. All city elections are nonpartisan. In most cities except for very large ones, the council members and the mayor are part-time positions. The constitution gives the voters in all cities the right to exercise the initiative and referendum, and to recall elected officers. Meetings of city councils and commissions or other advisory bodies must be open to the public.

In general law cities, a council of five, seven, or nine members is elected for four-year staggered terms. If the mayor is elected directly instead of being chosen by fellow council members, the term of office is two or four years, as determined by popular vote. The city clerk and treasurer also serve four-year terms. The chief of police and other department level heads are appointed by the city council or the city manager under merit system procedures.

Charter cities exhibit great variety in organization, being free to make any desired allocation of duties, powers, and functions between elective and appointive city officers. Charters may also provide for subgovernments in all or part of a city.

ADMINISTRATION

Two forms of administrative organization exist in California cities: the council-manager system and the mayor-council system. By modification and overlap these basic forms provide varied patterns of city government.

Council-manager. Three-fourths of California cities have some form of centralized professional administration. The administrator may be called a city manager, city administrator, or chief administrative officer. Under this type of administration, the elected council provides political leadership and makes policy, while a full-time professional manager directs city departments in carrying out that policy.

Mayor-council. In most California mayor-council cities, usually small general law communities, the mayor, chosen from among the council members, is merely the council's presiding officer and the city's ceremonial head. The council has substantial administrative as well as legislative power, with all department heads reporting directly to the council. This is the weak-mayor system. A number of cities, usually very large ones, use the strong-mayor system, though their charters set limits on how strong the mayor can be. In these cases the mayor is directly elected by the people. A chief administrative officer or general manager is in most matters responsible directly to the mayor, but may not be removed without the consent of the council. Top-level authority over some matters may be vested in independent boards or in elected officials. Under this system, the mayor's administrative authority depends in large part on his or her ability to elicit cooperation.

PLANNING

Municipal planning agencies are established in most cities and consist of a planning commission, the city council, a professional planning department, or a combination. All California cities must develop a general plan, consider environmental impact reports, and periodically review their capital improvements program.

The *planning commission* also has major responsibility for adoption and administration of zoning laws. The city council may, however, appoint a special board of zoning adjustment or an administrator to decide, subject to council review, on applications for conditional use or for variance from zoning requirements. Otherwise the planning commission itself acts on these matters, subject to council approval.

While the planning commission may also be concerned with the city's building regulations, sometimes a separate building commission formulates local building standards and approves applications for building permits.

Although renewal projects to clear and rebuild or rehabilitate blighted areas are determined locally, state law details the procedures to be used. A city may activate a *redevelopment agency* or local *housing authority* by an ordinance declaring the need for urban renewal or a housing program. Redevelopment is a big business in California, with nearly $4 billion in annual revenues. Over 90 percent of the medium and large-sized cities use redevelopment agencies. Their extraordinary powers, including eminent domain, often attract considerable controversy. The state constitution requires that local voters approve any public low-rent housing development before it may be undertaken.

BOARDS AND COMMISSIONS

Many city functions are overseen by various city boards and commissions, most of which are advisory to the city council. Some, however, are given quasi-judicial or limited administrative powers, subject to appeal to the council. Some city charters specifically establish citizen boards as part of the city administration, with independent authority and control of funds in their areas of operation.

Advisory boards or committees may be established by special ordinance, with their tasks reflecting community concerns. These bodies gather information on issues, hear arguments, weigh values, and recommend action to the council. Such boards may be permanent or may be assigned only one specific task. Except in very small communities, permanent commissions usually have the assistance of professional and clerical staff.

Besides the planning commission, some cities have a civil service or personnel board and probably a park and recreation commission. Cities may establish many other bodies such as a youth board, a solid waste management board, a traffic commission, an airport or harbor commission, or an art or historical commission.

A *civil service* or *personnel board* sets or recommends policy on employee compensation and working conditions, subject to state law. It hears appeals and grievances relating to city employment. Administration of a merit system for hiring and promoting is usually in the hands of a personnel director who works with the commission.

A *park and recreation commission* may be established to promote understanding among racial, religious, and age groups. Although these bodies are advisory, some play active roles in their communities. While they vary greatly in size, funding, and powers, a few have subpoena and hearing powers.

INTERGOVERNMENTAL COOPERATION

Cities do not stand alone. As part of an interlocking, governmental system, they have responsibilities to, and are affected by the actions of other levels of government, and work in cooperation with them on issues of concern to city residents.

CITY-COUNTY CONNECTIONS

Cities and counties have very strong ties. Cities benefit from county assessment rolls and county tax collection services. A county may provide money for city street construction that benefits the county's road system. The two jurisdictions often cooperate in building and operating parks, libraries, and other public facilities. City and county fire and law enforcement officers work together under mutual aid agreements, usually established for emergency situations.

The link between cities and counties is further strengthened by a constitutional provision permitting the legislature to require counties to perform specified services at the request of the cities within them.

The *Joint Exercise of Powers Act* is the legal basis for extensive contracting at the option of any two or more governmental units. To share costs, avoid duplicate efforts, or secure better facilities, cities often cooperate with other cities under this act, and frequently contract with special districts or counties for the purchase of services. In Los Angeles County such city-county contracts cover fire protection, law enforcement, jails, building inspection, personnel services, street sweeping, lighting, libraries, hospitals, animal control, and weed abatement. While the Los Angeles basin is the major location of such "contract" cities (cities that contract for nearly all services), selective contracting out is now widespread, especially since Proposition 13 in 1978. Cities contracting with their counties for most of their municipal services are said to operate under the Lakewood Plan.

CITY-STATE CONNECTIONS

All citizens, whether living in unincorporated territory or in cities, are subject to state law. City police enforce state laws along with municipal ordinances.

While city governments may affect local or municipal affairs, there are important limitations on their power to do so. Passage of local legislation must avoid conflicts with state law, and the state preempts power in issues of statewide concern. Local ordinances may not authorize acts prohibited by state statute, nor prohibit acts specifically authorized by the legislature.

Local ordinances are not applicable to state agencies unless the state consents—for example, the state consents to administer local sales taxes.

State preemption over local ordinance takes place in cases where the state is deemed to have broader authority in the field. For instance, by adopting the California Vehicle Code, the legislature has precluded cities from enacting their own traffic regulations except as expressly authorized in the state code. Cities are also preempted in the field of narcotics law and alcohol beverage control, with no exceptions. In many decisions the courts have invalidated local regulations based on their finding that the Legislature had the intent to preempt the field in question.

The state also sets standards in areas affecting the public health, safety, welfare, and environment. Although cities are allowed to exceed state standards, when a minimum standard is set by the state it is applicable to all cities. Exceptions are allowed in some instances—for example, in state building code requirements they are found necessary because of local conditions.

Cities receive substantial sums of money raised by the state from tax levies. The state also assesses the property of public utilities of local tax rolls. Special taxes must be expended for state or local purposes as specified by the legislature. For instance, gas tax funds must be used for construction and maintenance of city streets or for mass transit purposes. Vehicle fines must be spent for traffic control and traffic law enforcement.

The state also affects city government by granting or withholding funds, or prohibiting certain kinds of local taxation. Passage of the statewide initiative Proposition 13 in 1978 severely limited cities' ability to raise revenue based on property taxes. Cities may qualify for state grants for certain purposes.

A city may contract with the state for personnel services. Employees of many cities participate in the state system of retirement benefits.

CITY-FEDERAL CONNECTIONS

Because of the nature of the American governmental system, the federal government has little direct control over municipalities. Nevertheless, via the state or regional bodies, money from federal agencies reach local governments in the form of grants. Cities also benefit from direct federal grants and loans for community facilities and mass transportation, and from federal funding of redevelopment and housing agencies. Some federal control over cities is exerted through the criteria established for federal funding. Through these requirements the federal government may promote nondiscriminatory housing, environmental improvement, and citizen participation in governmental decision making.

17

SPECIAL DISTRICTS

Special districts are units of local government established by the residents of an area to provide some service not provided by the county or city. Within California there are 58 counties, 468 cities, and over 3,400 special districts, exclusive of school districts. **(See Chapter 14, The Educational System, for a discussion of school districts.)** California uses the special district form of local government on a wider scale than any other state in the nation.

Some special districts are located within cities. Many are located just outside city limits, in the unincorporated areas where one-quarter of the state's population lives. Suburban residents have often chosen to form special districts to provide needed services rather than form a city or annex their area to an existing city.

The size of the area served by a special district can vary tremendously. A lighting district, for instance, can be as small as one square block, while some water districts encompass several counties. Residents of many unincorporated areas are served by numerous special districts, each with its own set of boundaries.

In contrast to the broad constitutional and legal authority under which counties and cities operate, the authority of special districts is restricted to specifically enumerated powers and purposes. Special districts are limited in activity, in their ability to raise revenue, and in their power to regulate planning and land use.

ACTIVITIES

The first two special districts established in the state were irrigation districts, stemming from a need for affordable irrigation water in the San Joaquin Valley. By 1900, almost 50 irrigation districts had been formed to serve agricultural areas. Today, close to 900 special districts supply water to rural, suburban, and urban areas throughout the state.

In 1989-90, special districts engaged in 32 categories of activity. The frequency and variety of services provided by special districts are illustrated in **Figure 17.1.**

SPECIAL DISTRICT ACTIVITIES
1989-90

Number of Districts	Activity Category
890	Water utility
783	Lighting and lighting maintenance
586	Fire protection
577	Waste disposal (enterprise)
450	Streets and roads - construction and maintenance
410	Financing and constructing facilities
297	Recreation and park
260	Cemetery
216	Drainage and drainage maintenance
126	Land reclamation and levee maintenance
116	Resource conservation
47	Local and regional planning or development
41	Governmental services
97	Flood control and water conservation
79	Hospital
70	Pest control
71	Ambulance
55	Waste disposal (non-enterprise)
53	Transit
49	Police protection
37	Library services
34	Air pollution control
48	Electric
27	Memorial
11	Parking
13	Harbor and port
13	Television translator station facilities
17	Airport
8	Health
4	Animal control
5,485	Total

Note: Some districts engage in several activities; therefore the total number of activities reported (5,485) is greater than the total number of districts (3,440).

Source: State Controller's 1989-90 Annual Report

Figure 17.1

SINGLE-PURPOSE/MULTI-PURPOSE ACTIVITIES

Some special districts are authorized by law to perform a single function, others, to perform many activities. The vast majority are single-purpose districts: only ten percent, or about 500, are multi-purpose districts.

At one end of the spectrum are those districts which are exclusively single-purpose, such as street lighting districts. At the other end of the spectrum are districts whose permitted functions cover a full range of services, from safety and recreation services to water, sewage, and street lighting services. County service areas and community service districts which can provide a wide variety of services.

In between are many types of districts limited to a small set of closely related services with a concentration on just one of them. A familiar example is the fire protection district, formed primarily to prevent and suppress fires, but also authorized to provide ambulance service.

ENTERPRISE/NON-ENTERPRISE ACTIVITIES

Government activities are classified as either enterprise or non-enterprise, depending on the source of their funding.

Enterprise activities are financed entirely or predominantly by user fees set at a level to cover costs. Airports, harbors, hospitals, and water and sewer utilities, among others, are operated as special district enterprise activities. Special districts' enterprises generated over $6 billion in revenues in 1989-90.

Non-enterprise activities are supported primarily by generalized revenue sources. This form of district activity usually relies heavily on the property tax as a major source of revenue. Fire and police protection services are examples of non-enterprise activities.

As **Figure 17.2** illustrates, slightly more than half of the activities performed by special districts are enterprise in nature. Prior to 1978 both types of activities were growing at a six percent rate. When Proposition 13 caused a reduction in property tax support, the growth rate for non-enterprise activities slowed to four percent. Meanwhile, the number of enterprise activities continued to expand at the six percent growth rate, as districts turned to charging fees to cover costs, wherever possible. **(For more information on the financing of special districts, see Chapter 18, Budget and Finance.)**

GOVERNING BODIES

A special district is classified as either independent or dependent, according to the type of governing body under which it operates.

INDEPENDENT DISTRICT

An independent district operates under a locally elected, independent board of directors. About 66 percent of California's special districts are self-governed, independent districts.

DEPENDENT DISTRICT

A dependent district operates under the control of a county board of supervisors or a city council. On a statewide basis, 34 percent of the special districts are dependent in their governing structure. Most of these are governed by boards of supervisors. City councils and county supervisors often appoint local advisory boards to assist and advise them in governing dependent districts.

FORMATION AND CHANGE

Some counties encourage unincorporated communities to form independent districts when services are needed, so that local responsibility is maximized. Other counties prefer the formation of dependent districts, so that provision of services remains more firmly under county policy direction. Still other counties discourage the formation of special districts altogether, preferring that an area either annex itself to a city or form a new city to obtain needed services.

No special district may be formed without authorization by the state. The state legislature has authorized 55 general types of district formation and operation. Each type has its own unique subset of features in terms of the number and type of activities authorized, funding and taxing authority, and governing body. **Figure 17.2** illustrates the

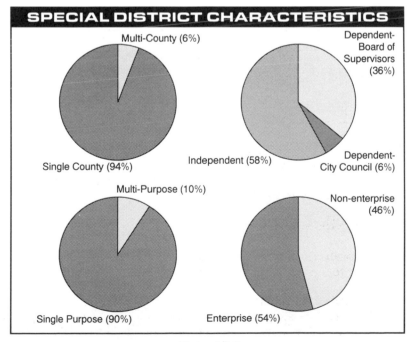

Figure 17.2

prevalence of the major characteristics on a statewide basis.

The procedures for defining and changing special district and city boundaries were standardized and consolidated by the legislature into the 1985 Cortese-Knox Local Government Reorganization Act. This law sets out uniform requirements for organizing a city or special district or initiating boundary changes. The act specifies what needs to be included in an application and petition, how many signatures are needed, how much public notice must be given, and when and how elections must be held.

LAFCO'S ROLE

Every county except San Francisco has a local agency formation commission. The LAFCO generally has five members: two county supervisors, two city council members, and one at-large or public member. Some LAFCOs add two representatives from independent special districts, for a total of seven members.

Formed by the legislature in 1963 to apply state policies and regulations, LAFCOs are legally independent of county, city, and special district governments. The legislature established a LAFCO in each county in an effort to discourage urban sprawl and ensure orderly formation and development of local governments.

To carry out this purpose, each commission has two main functions. One LAFCO responsibility is to determine the sphere of influence for each city and special district within the county. The sphere of influence is the delineated area into which each local agency can extend its services. This information helps a commission decide which configuration and type of agency is best suited to provide public services to a particular area.

The second major function of LAFCO is to review and act on requests to form or dissolve a local agency or to change the organization or boundaries of an existing agency. LAFCO must review any formal proposal for a new or reorganized unit of government or a boundary change.

The LAFCO staff considers the impact the proposal might have on the environment, on the residents of nearby areas, on other local agencies, and on the distribution of property tax. After evaluating costs, benefits, and public comments, the commission can take one of three actions: it can reject the proposal, approve it outright, or approve it subject to certain conditions or modifications.

BOARD OF SUPERVISORS' ROLE

Upon approval by LAFCO, a proposal to form or change a local government's boundaries or structure is sent to the county board of supervisors. The supervisors hold a public hearing and review any written protests. If there are no protests from a majority of the area's voters, the board places the issue on the ballot. Majority voter approval is required.

PAYING
FOR
GOVERNMENT

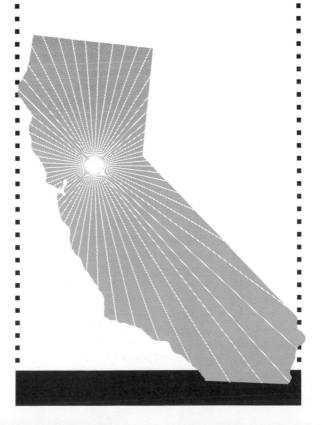

18

BUDGET
AND
FINANCE

Each level of government in California operates within a budget, which contains an estimate of available funds and revenues and a spending plan for a particular year. Nearly all levels of government consider July 1 the beginning of a budget or fiscal year and June 30 as the end of the fiscal year.

OVERVIEW OF GOVERNMENT BUDGETS

Like the federal government, the state government is not required to deliver a balanced budget. However, California has historically enacted a balanced budget. The federal government is much freer to borrow money; federal officials may deliberately plan to spend more than they expect to take in. The federal government is permitted to incur heavy, long-term debt in its efforts to influence the economy. At the state level, the governor must present a balanced budget proposal and must seek voter permission to issue bonds to borrow money against the General Fund.

Governments get their money from taxes, fees, the sale of bonds and from other levels of government. Very often the source of these revenues controls their use. For example, most of the money collected from motor vehicles taxes must, by law, be spent for transportation purposes. When the state allocates money to the counties or cities, certain restrictions are usually placed on how that money can be spent.

The funds from various revenue sources are separated into several categories. Money which is earmarked for a specific purpose is placed in a special revenue fund. The proceeds from each bond issued for a capital improvement go into a capital project fund. Revenues from self-supporting government operations are contained in enterprise funds. All revenues not earmarked for a specific purpose go into the General Fund.

Budgeting in any government is, to a great extent, automatic and mechanical. Budgets are based on historical information. Many obligations, such as for debt service, are legally required. Retirement and other fringe benefits secured by contracts with government employees must be paid, along with utility costs. Money designated for

CALIFORNIA BUDGET PROCESS

EXECUTIVE BRANCH		LEGISLATIVE BRANCH
Administrative departments prepare budgetary requests.	APRIL	
Agencies prepare preliminary program budgets.	MAY	
Department of Finance and governor issue policy directions.	JULY AUGUST	
Department of Finance reviews agency proposals.	SEPTEMBER OCTOBER	
Commission on State Finance and experts forecast revenues.	NOVEMBER	
Governor finalizes budget and sends it to the state printing office.	JANUARY	
JAN. 10: Governor submits budget to legislature.		Fiscal committee chairs introduce governor's proposal as budget bill.
	FEBRUARY	Legislative analyst studies proposed budget; issues *Analysis of Budget Bill* and *Perspectives and Issues.*
	MARCH APRIL	Assembly and Senate budget subcommittees hold public hearings on assigned sections of the budget.
Department of Finance issues revised forecast of revenues and expenditures.	MAY	Subcommittees complete action on budget.
		Full budget committees hold hearings and vote.
		Assembly and Senate pass respective versions of the budget bill.
	JUNE	Conference committee of 3 Assembly members and 3 senators agree on a compromise budget bill.
		JUNE 15: Legislature submits approved budget to governor.
JUNE 30: Governor exercises line item veto and signs budget act.		
	JULY	Legislature can restore vetoed items by two-thirds vote in each house.

Figure 18.1

certain programs or services must be spent for those purposes. The effects of inflation require cost-of-living adjustments (COLAs) merely to maintain the same levels of services. In practice, COLAs are governed by statute. Statutes can be, and usually are, subject to change.

Consequently, only a portion of a jurisdiction's General Fund is actually available for discretionary spending. There is relatively little change in existing ones, depending on the agenda of the current administration. This discretionary portion of the General Fund is the focus of most of the debate during the budget process.

STATE BUDGET PROCESS

All three of the branches of government have roles in the process leading to the adoption of the budget. In California this process consumes a full fourteen months. In May and June, planning is underway for the fiscal year that will begin July 1 of the succeeding calendar year.

GOVERNOR'S PROPOSAL

During the spring months each administrative department prepares its budgetary requests. Instead of detailing the amounts item by item, each agency classifies expenditures according to the programs for which they will be spent. Using this program format, required by law since 1978, a department shows what services it provides and how much each service costs. The salaries, supplies, and overhead for the department as a whole are distributed into each program's costs on a percentage basis.

In July, the Department of Finance and the governor issue instructions and policy directions on extending services or limiting spending. In autumn, the agency secretaries review the preliminary budgets of departments within their jurisdiction. Internal budget hearings are sometimes necessary to resolve competing demands for the dollars available. The Department of Finance reviews each agency proposal and makes its own revenue projections which are used in the preparation of the governor's budget.

In November, state revenue forecasters confer with selected economists, business experts, and labor leaders. Data from many sources is closely analyzed in order to estimate revenues for the following fiscal year.

The Commission on State Finance, an independent nonpartisan commission created by law in 1979, projects expenditures remaining in the current year, any anticipated surplus or deficit, and state revenues. (The commission must make such forecasts at least four times a year.) The conditions of the national economy and their implications for California are taken into account. The forecast includes an estimate of revenues from such major sources as the personal income tax, corporate income tax, and sales tax. The proposals for spending are then tailored to fit within the constraints of the estimated revenues. The Commission on State Finance and the Department of Finance are not affiliated and frequently dispute each other's revenue projections.

Eventually a budget outline with a variety of options is forwarded from the Department of Finance to the governor. The governor decides which items to include. If the proposed spending level is greater than estimated revenues, the governor must either recommend tax changes or other specific sources of income to make up the difference, or reduce the proposed spending level so the budget is balanced. The governor's proposed package is then sent to the state printing office in early January. On or before January 10, the governor goes before the legislature to deliver a State of the State address which includes highlights of the proposed budget. The state constitution requires the governor to submit a balanced budget to the legislature by the tenth day of January.

THE LEGISLATURE AND THE BUDGET

In order for the legislature to consider the governor's proposed budget, the budget must be put in the form of a bill introduced by the chairs of the Budget Committee of each house. In the Assembly, the budget bill is introduced by the chair of the Ways and Means Committee, in the Senate by the chair of the Budget and Fiscal Review Committee.

The legislative analyst's office reviews the governor's proposals. By the end of February the legislative analyst has completed a comprehensive study of the proposed budget and the underlying economic assumptions. An *Analysis of the Budget Bill* and a companion document, *Perspectives and Issues*, are published and submitted to the members of the legislature. Together these reports total close to two thousand pages.

The legislative analyst plays a key role in the budget process as the legislature's main financial adviser. The *Analysis of the Budget Bill* discusses selected programs that are funded from the General Fund. The analysis indicates the dollar amount and percentage of any proposed increase or decrease from the previous year's spending. This is followed by a general program statement, an overview and evaluation of the budget request, and the analyst's recommendations for future spending. The analyst's recommendation may differ considerably from the governor's proposals. A program which is criticized by the legislative analyst often turns into a controversial budget program.

The legislative analyst can also suggest that certain portions of the tax structure be carefully scrutinized. The analyst's recommendation may be to change a particular tax rate or to modify or eliminate certain tax exemptions, deductions, exclusions, or credits, since each such tax exemption represents lost revenue. Since the passage of Proposition 13 in 1978, a two-thirds vote of each house is required to impose any new tax. A tax exemption can be granted by a majority vote of the legislature; its repeal requires a two-thirds vote. In 1985, the legislature adopted a formal process for reviewing tax exemptions.

The fiscal committee of each house is divided into budget subcommittees, which conduct public hearings on assigned sections of the budget, usually in March, April, and May. Any private citizen, interest group, legislative advocate, or government staff member may address a budget subcommittee to advocate a higher or lower spending level for a particular program.

In May, the Department of Finance presents an updated estimate of program needs and revenues needed for the rest of the current fiscal year and a refined forecast of revenues and expenditures; the subcommittees review and integrate their recommendations accordingly.

The decisions of the budget subcommittees are significant. Traditionally, the full committees accept the subcommittee recommendations without alteration; only a few items are debated and changed by the full committees.

A budget bill, reflecting all changes that have been made in committees, is then sent to the floor of each house. This is where first public debate is seen. Each house passes its own version of the budget bill and sends it to the other house for consideration. Each house traditionally votes to reject the other's version, triggering the need for a conference committee.

The budget conference committee consists of three Senate and three Assembly members. Responsibility for chairing the conference committee alternates annually between both houses. The Senate and Assembly each prepare their own version of the budget bill. The conference committee holds public hearings during June and attempts to resolve the differences between the two versions of the budget. Each house must approve a compromise budget by a two-thirds vote. According to the constitution, the legislature must submit an approved budget to the governor by June 15. However, in years past this has not been the case. Since 1971, with the exception of five budget proposals, the legislature has not submitted an approved budget to the governor by the deadline date.

ADOPTION OF THE BUDGET

The Governor has until June 30, or 12 days after the passage of the conference committee report (i.e., budget bill), whichever is the earliest, to decide what do with the budget bill. Though permitted, the governor almost never signs or vetoes the budget bill in its entirety, but uses the line item veto to reduce or eliminate specific items. The legislature has the next sixty days that it is in session to override a line item veto by a two-thirds vote of each house. The governor's veto of a budget item is rarely overridden by the legislature.

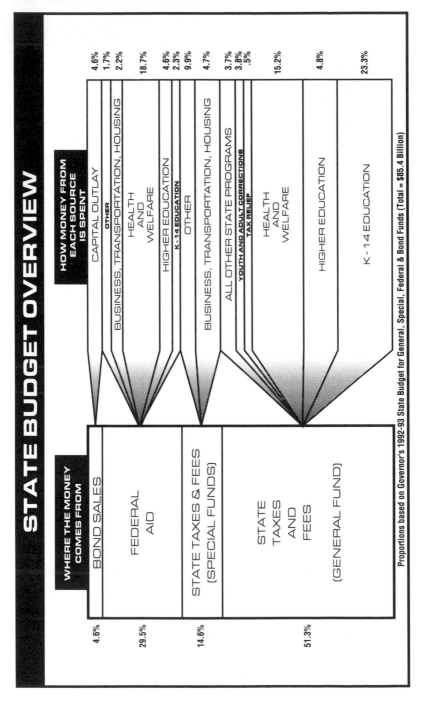

Figure 18.2

STATE INCOME

California derives its income from its own taxes and fees, from the federal government, and from the sale of bonds. In 1992-93, state taxes and fees will constitute approximately 66 percent of the state's income; federal aid 29 percent; bond sales five percent. **(See Figure 18.3.)**

GENERAL FUND

About 78 percent of the proceeds from taxes and fees (excluding transfers) imposed by the state go into the General Fund. The remaining 22 percent are special fund revenues. The three largest General Fund revenue sources are the personal tax, the sales and use tax, and the bank and corporation tax.

The *personal income tax* was implemented in 1935 and is the single largest General Fund revenue source (43 percent). The tax is on personal income and the tax rates range from one to eleven percent. The tax rate brackets, standard deduction, and personal and dependent credits are based on June California Consumer Price Index. This tax is administered by the Franchise Tax Board.

The *sales and use tax* was implemented in 1933 and is the second single largest General Fund revenue source (37 percent). The state government and local governments share this tax. Currently, the state's rate is six percent while local rates may vary from 1.25 percent to 2.75 percent. The tax is imposed on sales of tangible property, but there are numerous exclusions including food for home consumption, prescription medications, gas, electricity, and relief from a variety of sales ranging from custom computer programs to aircraft. This tax is administered by the Board of Equalization.

The *bank and corporation tax* was implemented in 1929 and is the third largest General Fund revenue (12 percent). The tax is imposed on corporate income attributable to California activities at a tax rate of 9.3 percent. California taxable income is determined using a three-factor formula based on sales, payroll, and property value. International corporations may elect special treatment but must pay a special fee. An additional 1.7 percent rate is applied to financial institutions (banks and savings and loans) in lieu of personal property taxes and business license fees. This tax is administered by the Franchise Tax Board.

The insurance gross premiums tax, estate taxes, cigarette tax, alcoholic beverage taxes, and horse racing fees account for about five percent of General Fund revenues. Additional licenses and fees and fund transfers contribute three percent.

The inheritance and gift taxes were repealed by the voters in 1982, and the estate tax was imposed in their place. This allows the state to receive a portion of the federal estate tax at no increased cost to the taxpayer.

SPECIAL FUNDS

About 22 percent of state revenue goes into special funds. The use of money in a special fund is restricted by law for particular purposes.

The California Constitution, codes and statutes specify the uses for certain revenue. Such receipts are accounted for in various special funds. In general, special fund revenues comprise three categories of income:

- receipts from tax levies which are allocated to specified functions, such as motor vehicle taxes and fees
- charges for special services to specific functions, including such items as business and professional license fees
- rental royalties and other receipts designated for a particular purpose—for example, oil and gas royalties.

Motor vehicle related taxes and fees account for 54 percent of all special fund revenue. Principal sources of this income are motor vehicle fuel taxes, registration and weight fees, and vehicle license fees. During the 1991-92 fiscal year, $6.2 billion will be derived from the ownership or operation of motor vehicles. Approximately $3.8 billion of this revenue will be returned to local governments. The remainder will be available for various state programs related to transportation and services to vehicle owners.

Chapter 85, Statutes of 1991, created a new special fund for the purpose of local program realignment. Revenue attributable to a half-cent sales tax rate was transferred to this Local Revenue Fund. During 1991-92, it is estimated that local governments will receive almost $1.6 billion from this revenue source. In addition to this revenue, approximately 25 percent of all vehicle license fees are transferred to this fund.

Funds from the voter-approved increase in tobacco related taxes (Proposition 99) are allocated to a special fund for distribution to a variety of accounts as determined by the measure. Receipts for this fund are estimated at $495 million in 1992-93. The original 10 cents per package tax on cigarettes is allocated to the General Fund and a special fund for distribution to cities. It is estimated that the cities will receive $30 million during 1991-92 and $29 million in 1992-93.

FEDERAL FUNDS

The money that comes to the state treasury from Washington is placed into special accounts. The federal dollars are then redistributed to programs and individuals as required by federal laws and regulations.

The amount of federal aid received by California has been very volatile during the past fifteen years. State expenditure of federal funds have ranged from a decrease of 9.4 percent to an annual increase of 25.6 percent. The average has increased 7.8 percent since 1977. Any efforts by Washington officials to reduce the federal budget deficit could result in a significant reduction of federal money received by state and local agencies.

STATE GENERAL FUND REVENUES AND TRANSFERS 1992-93 FISCAL YEAR

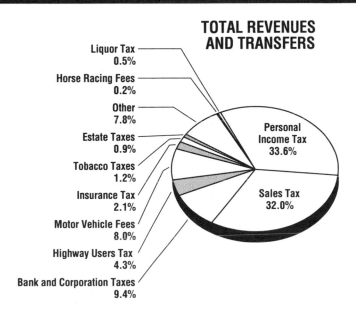

TOTAL REVENUES AND TRANSFERS

Liquor Tax
0.5%

Horse Racing Fees
0.2%

Other
7.8%

Estate Taxes
0.9%

Tobacco Taxes
1.2%

Insurance Tax
2.1%

Motor Vehicle Fees
8.0%

Highway Users Tax
4.3%

Bank and Corporation Taxes
9.4%

Personal Income Tax
33.6%

Sales Tax
32.0%

GENERAL FUND REVENUES AND TRANSFERS

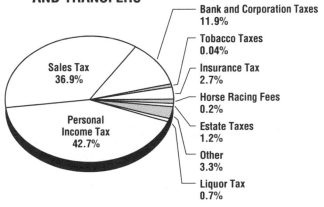

Bank and Corporation Taxes
11.9%

Tobacco Taxes
0.04%

Insurance Tax
2.7%

Horse Racing Fees
0.2%

Estate Taxes
1.2%

Other
3.3%

Liquor Tax
0.7%

Sales Tax
36.9%

Personal Income Tax
42.7%

Source: Governor's Budget Summary 1992-93

Figure 18.3

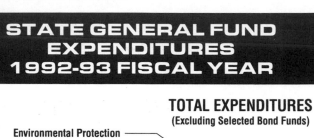

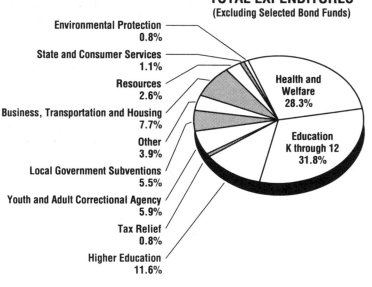

TOTAL EXPENDITURES
(Excluding Selected Bond Funds)

Environmental Protection
0.8%

State and Consumer Services
1.1%

Resources
2.6%

Business, Transportation and Housing
7.7%

Other
3.9%

Local Government Subventions
5.5%

Youth and Adult Correctional Agency
5.9%

Tax Relief
0.8%

Higher Education
11.6%

Health and Welfare
28.3%

Education K through 12
31.8%

GENERAL FUND EXPENDITURES

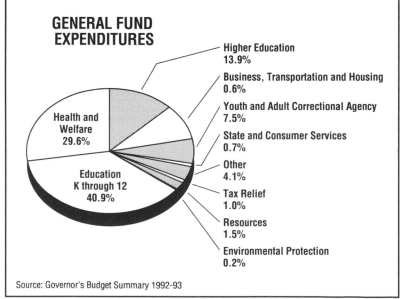

Higher Education
13.9%

Business, Transportation and Housing
0.6%

Youth and Adult Correctional Agency
7.5%

State and Consumer Services
0.7%

Other
4.1%

Tax Relief
1.0%

Resources
1.5%

Environmental Protection
0.2%

Health and Welfare
29.6%

Education K through 12
40.9%

Source: Governor's Budget Summary 1992-93

Figure 18.4

BONDS

The state budget for a given fiscal year anticipates income from the sale of bonds; the amount anticipated varies depending on the number of bonds that have been authorized for sale and their relative attractiveness to investors. Much more in proceeds from bond sales has been realized in recent years from the sale of revenue bonds than from the sale of general obligation bonds.

Among the mechanisms used by the state to borrow large sums of money, the state bond program is the most important one needed to purchase, build, or develop major facilities such as parklands and school facilities. Further information about bonds can be found in **Figure 18.5.**

ABOUT BONDS

Bond. An interest-bearing certificate issued by the government as a promise to repay a loan to the government at the end of a specified period, usually 20 or 30 years. The purchaser of the bond is lending money to the government. The government periodically pays bond purchasers a specified interest rate. The holder of the bond does not have to pay income tax on the interest received.

Revenue Bond. A bond repaid using money earned by the project which was financed by that bond. For example, rent received for college dormitories goes towards the repayment of the bond sold to build the dorms. There is no ceiling on the interest rate that the government may offer the lender. State revenue bonds must be authorized by a majority vote of both houses of the legislature. Voter authorization is not required.

General Obligation Bond. A bond repaid using money from the General Fund. State general obligation bonds must be authorized by a two-thirds vote of both houses of the legislature and a majority vote of the people.

Counties, cities, and special districts are also authorized to issue general obligation bonds. Local governments traditionally raised the property tax to finance repayment of bonds. However, since Proposition 13 in 1978 fixed the property tax rate at one percent and local governments can no longer adjust that rate, their ability to issue general obligation bonds has been effectively eliminated.

Special Assessment Bond. Sold by counties, cities and special districts to finance public works projects like streets and sewers. Each landowner in the area served by the capital improvement pays an amount based on the share of the benefit received by that parcel of property.

Bond Rating. A government bond is rated by a rating agency at the time of sale as to its soundness as an investment. The rating on a general obligation bond depends on the ability of the state to raise sufficient revenues to assure regular payments to the purchaser of the bond. The lower the rating the higher the interest the taxpayer pays. Over the past decade, California's general obligation bonds have been rated both AA+ and AAA, although the state has predominantly maintained a triple A rating.

Figure 18.5

STATE EXPENDITURES

Since the passage of Proposition 4 in November 1979, which was amended by Propositions 98 and 111, state and local government spending has been under certain constitutional controls. The voters approved the three main provisions:

- The spending level of tax dollars is limited; it is tied to changes in population and the cost of living from year to year.
- Government cannot keep surplus funds. Any funds, in excess of the State Appropriations Limit are averaged over two years and any surplus must be returned to the taxpayers or go to K-14 education within two years.
- When the state requires local government to provide certain programs or services (mandates), the state must pay local government to cover the associated costs.

The California budget has two major spending categories. Nearly 32 percent of the total state budget is spent for education; 28 percent, for health and welfare. Each of these broad spending programs is paid for by a combination of state General Fund, special funds and federal revenue sources. **(see Figure 18.4)**

EXPENDITURES FROM THE GENERAL FUND

General Fund expenditures account for about one-half of all spending under the auspices of state government.

The largest programs supported by the General Fund are education and health and welfare. Approximately 84 percent of General Fund dollars goes to K-12 and higher education and to health and welfare benefits. These have been the fastest growing components of General Fund expenditures in recent years.

The remainder of the General Fund money goes for tax relief and other programs of state government, such as resources and youth and adult corrections. General Fund expenditures encompass the following:

Aid to local government. Seventy-six percent of the General Fund money goes to local government assistance; by contrast, the amount that went to local government before 1978 was about a third of the General Fund. The dramatic growth in financial relief to local governments reflects state actions taken following the passage of Proposition 13, which limited governments' ability to raise money through property taxes. This spending category includes payment to local government for programs and services mandated by the state. State grants for various programs are another form of local assistance. Included in this category of expenditures is aid to individual Californians who qualify for certain assistance or benefit payments. This spending category represents payments through programs such as Medi-Cal, Aid to Families with Dependent Children, Social Security Insurance, and homeowners' and renters' tax credit. Most of this money is passed through to the counties (in the form of local assistance) for distribution to individual recipients.

State operations. The remainder of the General Fund pays for day-to-day operating costs of state government, such as salaries, benefits, and office supplies. Of this quarter, over 37 percent is expended for the support of the higher education segment.

Special Fund Reserve for economic uncertainties. This fund was created to provide a source of funds to meet General Fund obligations in the event of financial emergencies and cash-flow shortages.

EXPENDITURES FROM SPECIAL FUNDS

In recent years special fund expenditures have represented 13 to 15 percent of the total spending plan. Each earmarked fund pays for the program or service for which the account was established. Local governments' share of the motor vehicle license and registration fees, gas tax, sales tax, cigarette tax, and tidelands oil and gas revenues are paid out of special funds.

Thirty-four percent of the proceeds from the California State Lottery, approved by the voters in November 1984, is distributed from a separate fund, on a per capita basis, to K-12 education, community colleges, and the two university systems.

EXPENDITURES FROM FEDERAL FUNDS

Most recently, expenditures from federal funds have represented approximately one quarter of the total annual outgo from the state treasury.

More than half of the federal dollars are paid out to individuals in California who are eligible for health and welfare benefits such as AFDC, and Unemployment Insurance. The actual amount passing through the California treasury varies according to the number of Californians meeting eligibility requirements at any given time.

About one-quarter of the funds received from Washington are designated for use in education programs. In recent years nearly one-tenth of the federal aid has been earmarked for particular transportation, housing and business programs. State officials have little or no discretion in how these federal dollars will be spent.

EXPENDITURES FROM BOND FUNDS

Proceeds from the sales of bonds are spent on the projects for which they were specifically authorized. The largest expenditures in recent years have been for state prison and county jail construction, the lease-purchase of school buildings, construction of facilities for clean and safe drinking water, and parklands acquisition and development. In any given year, the amount spent on these projects represents approximately three percent of total state expenditures.

ABOUT PROPERTY TAXES

Real property. Land and improvements that are permanently attached, such as buildings and houses, including mobile homes located on permanent foundations. Subject to the property tax. Real property owned by a church, governmental entity, or bank is exempt from the property tax.

Personal property. Movable, unsecured property. Includes business furnishings and equipment, boats, aircraft, and railroad cars. Excludes home furnishings and business inventories.

Full cash value. Market value. The highest amount a willing and knowledgeable seller of property could obtain from a willing and knowledgeable buyer.

Assessed value. Set at full cash value as of 1975-76; under Proposition 13, growth in the assessed value is restricted to a two percent annual increase. Real property is only reassessed to reflect full cash value of new construction or the full cash value at the time of the sale or change of ownership. About 18 percent of all properties statewide change hands in a given year and thus are reassessed to current value.

Tax rate. Limited by Proposition 13 to one percent of assessed value. Cannot exceed $1 per $100 of assessed valuation where needed to pay off bonds and other debts approved by the voters prior to July 1, 1978.

Board of Equalization. Responsible for standardizing assessment practices within and among California's 58 counties. Grants property tax exemptions for property dedicated to health, educational, and charitable purposes.

Figure 18.6

LOCAL GOVERNMENT BUDGETS

Of all the public dollars spent in California, almost three out of four are spent at the local level of government. There are about 8,000 units of local government in California, including counties, cities, special districts, community redevelopment agencies, school and community college districts. Their budgets are matters of public record and are subject to public hearings before adoption by the governing boards.

State and federal funds, passed down to local governments for disbursement, provide a great portion of their income. For additional money to provide services, local governments have traditionally relied heavily on the property tax, the oldest form of taxation. The limitations placed on the property tax by Proposition 13 in 1978 have forced local governments to reduce reliance on property tax revenue and increase reliance on other revenue sources.

FINANCING COUNTIES

General revenues come into county coffers from a variety of sources, with state and federal government providing more than half of the total. For example, in 1989-90, the amount collected at the state level that was passed down to the counties for disbursement represented about 37 percent of county revenues; the amount from the federal level, 18 percent, for a total of 55 percent. Unlike cities, counties may levy only those taxes expressly permitted by the legislature, and then, only in unincorporated areas.

Property taxes in 1989-90 constituted about 24 percent of total county revenues. Prior to Proposition 13, counties had relied on property taxes for close to 35 percent of their budgets. Most of the counties' lost property tax revenues was made up by an increase in state aid.

Fees are charged by counties to help defray the costs of certain services. Examples include court fees, recording fees, health service fees, and park and recreation fees. The money generated by these represented about eight percent of the 1989-90 county revenues.

The money collected from licenses, permits, franchises, fines, vehicle and court fines, penalties, rents, and royalties constituted six percent of 1989-90 county revenues. The sales, room occupancy, transportation, and other local taxes accounted for the remaining seven percent.

A portion of each county's income and spending is related to enterprise activities which are essentially self-supporting. Counties charge fees to offset the cost of services such as hospitals, airports, refuse collection, harbors, parking, water, and sanitation.

The major spending categories in county budgets are illustrated by the following table of the 1989-90 expenditures, as reported by the state controller:

    40%   Public Assistance
    29%   Public Protection
           (judicial, police, fire, detention and correction, flood
           control, soil conservation, etc.)
    14%   General
           (administrative, personnel, election, etc.)
    11%   Health and Sanitation
     3%   Public Roads and Transportation Facilities
     3%   Education, Recreation and Culture, and Debt Service

FINANCING CITIES

Charter cities are authorized by the constitution to impose any tax not specifically prohibited by the state. General law cities may levy only those taxes expressly permitted by the legislature. However, the legislature has extended the taxing authority held by charter cities to general law cities.

The tax rates for locally imposed taxes are set by the local government. For example, city councils can vary the rates of business licenses, hotel taxes, charges for municipal services, and fees for development permits.

Cities have greater flexibility than counties in their ability to produce revenue. Cities have access to about 20 kinds of tax and non-tax funds from local, state, and federal sources. They rely heavily on locally imposed service charges and taxes to pay for municipal operations. Local revenue sources constitute about 72 percent of total revenue service; service charges bring in about 38 percent; taxes, 34 percent.

Electric service charges, water service and connection fees, and sewer service and connection fees are the major types of service charges. Lesser amounts come from solid waste revenues, airport, port and harbor revenues, and gas revenues.

The sales and use tax and the property tax provide the principal portion of city tax funds. Other sources of tax revenue include the transportation tax, business license tax, and utility users tax.

Money collected at the federal and state levels and forwarded to cities for disbursement accounts for about ten percent of city budgets. Community development block grants provide the principal federal revenues. The state money represents the cities' portion of the state gasoline tax, motor vehicle in-lieu tax, property tax relief, and cigarette tax.

Other municipal revenue sources include investment earnings, rents, special benefits assessments, licenses and permits, and fines and forfeitures.

The precise amount spent for a particular program or service varies from city to city. The major spending categories for 1989-90, as reported by the state controller were as follows:

26%   Public Safety
       (police, fire, street lighting, emergency medical, etc.)
24%   Public Utilities
       (electric, water, gas)
18%   Community Development/Health
       (planning, construction and engineering regulation, etc.)
14%   Transportation
       (streets, highways, storm drains, airports, ports and
       harbors, public transit, etc.)
10%   Culture and Leisure
 7%   General Government
       (administrative and management support)
 1%   Other

Borrowing authority is an essential source of support for capital improvements. Cities have the legal authority to issue both revenue and general obligation bonds, as well as lease-purchase bonds, which are repayable by revenues from facility rentals.

FINANCING SPECIAL DISTRICTS

Special districts rely primarily on three local revenue sources: user charges or service fees, property taxes, and special assessments. The level of dependence on one or more of them varies according to the kind of district and type of service provided. Enterprise activities such as water supply and sewage disposal are supported entirely by user charges or service fees.

In contrast, non-enterprise special districts such as fire protection and parks and recreation districts, rely heavily on property taxes for revenues. Prior to Proposition 13, the property tax was the source of close to three-quarters of their revenues; now the property tax provides about one-quarter of their revenues.

State government has made up about 19 percent of property tax shortfalls by providing the Special District Augmentation Fund, distributed to special districts at the discretion of the county board of supervisors. Non-enterprise districts have also turned to operating a greater number of programs and services on a self-supporting basis, charging the individual user a fee high enough to pay for the full cost the program, rather than subsidizing the service with general tax dollars.

With few exceptions, special districts are authorized to borrow money for major construction projects by issuing bonds, subject to voter approval. Revenue and lease-purchase bonds are the prevalent types being issued.

ABBREVIATIONS and ACRONYMS

AB	**A**ssembly **B**ill
ABAG	**A**ssociation of **B**ay **A**rea **G**overnments
ACA	**A**ssembly **C**onstitutional **A**mendment
ACR	**A**ssembly **C**oncurrent **R**esolution
ADA	**A**verage **D**aily **A**ttendance
AFDC	**A**id to **F**amilies with **D**ependent **C**hildren
AG	**A**ttorney **G**eneral
AJR	**A**ssembly **J**oint **R**esolution
ALRB	**A**gricultural **L**abor **R**elations **B**oard
APCD	**A**ir **P**ollution **C**ontrol **D**istrict
AQMD	**A**ir **Q**uality **M**anagement **D**istrict
ARB	**A**ir **R**esources **B**oard
BCDC	S.F. **B**ay **C**onservation and **D**evelopment **C**ommission
Cal-DOSH	**Cal**ifornia **O**ccupational **S**afety and **H**ealth
Caltrans	**Cal**ifornia Department of **Trans**portation
CEQA	**C**alifornia **E**nvironmental **Q**uality **A**ct
COFPHE	**C**apital **O**utlay **F**und for **P**ublic **H**igher **E**ducation ("Coffee" Fund)
COLA	**C**ost **o**f **L**iving **A**djustment
CPUC	**C**alifornia **P**ublic **U**tilities **C**ommission
CSU	**C**alifornia **S**tate **U**niversity
DI	**D**isability **I**nsurance
DMH	**D**epartment of **M**ental **H**ealth
DPA	**D**epartment of **P**ersonnel **A**dministration
DSS	**D**epartment of **S**ocial **S**ervices
DWR	**D**epartment of **W**ater **R**esources
EDD	**E**mployment **D**evelopment **D**epartment
EIR	**E**nvironmental **I**mpact **R**eport
EMS	**E**mergency **M**edical **S**ervices
FPPC	**F**air **P**olitical **P**ractices **C**ommission
FTB	**F**ranchise **T**ax **B**oard
GAIN	**G**reater **A**venues for **In**dependence
JTPA	**J**ob **T**raining **P**artnership **A**ct
K-12	**K**indergarten through **12**th grade
LAFCO	**L**ocal **A**gency **F**ormation **Co**mmission
LCP	**L**ocal **C**oastal **P**rogram
OAL	**O**ffice of **A**dministrative **L**aw
OCJP	**O**ffice of **C**riminal **J**ustice **P**lanning
OPR	**O**ffice of **P**lanning and **R**esearch
PAC	**P**olitical **A**ction **C**ommittee
PERB	**P**ublic **E**mployment **R**elations **B**oard
PERS	**P**ublic **E**mployees' **R**etirement **S**ystem
SACOG	**S**acramento **A**rea **C**ouncil **o**f **G**overnments
SANDAG	**San D**iego **A**ssociation of **G**overnments
SB	**S**enate **B**ill
SCA	**S**enate **C**onstitutional **A**mendment
SCAG	**S**outhern **C**alifornia **A**ssociation of **G**overnments
SCR	**S**enate **C**oncurrent **R**esolution
SJR	**S**enate **J**oint **R**esolution
SSI	**S**upplemental **S**ecurity **I**ncome
SSP	**S**tate **S**upplemental **P**ayment
STRS	**S**tate **T**eachers' **R**etirement **S**ystem
TRPA	**T**ahoe **R**egional **P**lanning **A**gency
UC	**U**niversity of **C**alifornia
UI	**U**nemployment **I**nsurance

Prepared by League of Women Voters of California

SOURCES OF FURTHER INFORMATION

GOVERNMENT SOURCES

Assembly Office of Research
1020 N Street, Suite 408
Sacramento, CA 95814

Office of the Auditor General
660 J Street, #300
Sacramento, CA 95814

Business, Transportation, and Housing Agency
1120 N Street, Suite 2101
Sacramento, CA 95814

California Environmental Protection Agency
555 Capitol Mall, Suite 235
Sacramento, CA 95814

Department of Justice (Attorney General)
1515 K Street
Sacramento, CA 95814

Fair Political Practices Commission
428 J Street
Sacramento, CA 95814

Health and Welfare Agency
1600 Ninth Street, Room 460
Sacramento, CA 95814

Office of the Legislative Analyst
925 L Street, #650
Sacramento, CA 95814

Judicial Council of California, Administrative Office of the Courts
303 Second Street, South Tower
San Francisco, CA 94107

Resources Agency
1416 Ninth Street, Suite 1311
Sacramento, CA 95814

Secretary of State
1230 J Street
Sacramento, CA 95814
(for information relating to elections,
campaign disclosure, and lobbyist registration)

Senate Office of Research
1020 N Street, Suite 565
Sacramento, CA 95814

State and Consumer Services Agency
915 Capitol Mall, Suite 200
Sacramento, CA 95814

State Library
914 Capitol Mall
Sacramento, CA 95814

Youth and Adult Correctional Agency
1100 Eleventh Street, Suite 400
Sacramento, CA 95814

Governor
State Capitol
Sacramento, CA 95814

Lieutenant Governor
State Capitol
Sacramento, CA 95814

Treasurer
915 Capitol Mall, #110
Sacramento, CA 95814

Controller
300 Capitol Mall, 18th Floor
Sacramento, CA 95814

Superintendent of Public Education
721 Capitol Mall
Sacramento, CA 95814

Insurance Commissioner
770 L Street, Suite 1120
Sacramento, CA 95814

Assembly Member (name or district number)
State Capitol
Sacramento, CA 95814

State Senator (name or district number)
State Capitol
Sacramento, CA 95814

Board of Equalization
1020 N Street, Room 112
Sacramento, CA 95814

ORGANIZATIONS

California Tax Reform Association
926 J Street, #913
Sacramento, CA 95814

California Taxpayers Association
921 Eleventh Street, Suite 800
Sacramento, CA 95814

California State Association of Counties
1100 K Street, #101
Sacramento, CA 95814

California Association of Councils of Government
1100 Eleventh Street, #305
Sacramento, CA 95814

California State University (CSU) Governmental Affairs
925 L Street, #200
Sacramento, CA 95814

EdSource
525 Middlefield Road, Suite 100
Menlo Park, CA 94025

Institute of Governmental Affairs
Shields Library - University of California, Davis
Davis, CA 95616

Institute of Governmental Affairs
128 Moses Hall - University of California, Berkeley
Berkeley, CA 94270

League of California Cities
1400 K Street
Sacramento, CA 95814

University of California (UC) Governmental Affairs
1130 K Street, #340
Sacramento, CA 95814

INFORMATION ON CURRENT YEAR

California County Fact Book, California State Association of Counties, 1100 K Street, #101, Sacramento, CA 95814.

California Journal Roster & Government Guide,
1714 Capitol Avenue, Sacramento, CA 95814.

Department of General Services, ***Publications Catalogue***, Department of General Services, Procurement Unit, P.O. Box 1015,
North Highlands, CA 95660.

Governor's Budget for (year), ***Salaries and Wages Supplement***,
Legislative Bill Room, State Capitol, Sacramento, CA 95814.

Governor's Budget Summary (year), Legislative Bill Room,
State Capitol, Sacramento, CA 95814.

Handbook of the California Legislature, Legislative Bill Room, State Capitol, Sacramento, CA 95814

Legislative Analyst, *Analysis of the Budget Bill of the State of California for Fiscal Year...*, Legislative Bill Room, State Capitol, Sacramento, CA 95814.

Legislative Analyst, *The* (year) *Budget: Perspectives and Issues*, Legislative Bill Room, State Capitol, Sacramento, CA 95814.

Secretary of State, *A Study of California Ballot Measures 1884 to 1990*, Office of the Secretary of State, 1230 J Street, Sacramento, CA 95814.

State Controller, *Annual Reports of Financial Transactions Concerning Cities, Counties, Public Retirement Systems, School Districts, Special Districts, Streets and Roads* (six separate reports), Office of the State Controller, Local Government Fiscal Affairs, P.O. Box 1019, Sacramento, CA 95805.

State Library, *California State Publications* (a listing of newly released departmental reports and other state publications, published monthly with annual cumulative listing; available in many libraries), 914 Capitol Mall, Sacramento, CA 95814.

OTHER PUBLICATIONS AND DOCUMENTS

A Fist Full of Dollars, July 1991, California Common Cause, 926 J Street, Sacramento, CA 95814.

California Codes of Law: Education, Elections, Government, Health and Safety, Insurance, Labor, Unemployment Insurance, Welfare and Institutions. Separate volumes, published every other year, with supplements in the intervening year. Department of General Services, Publications Unit, P.O. Box 1015, North Highlands, CA 95660.

California Government and Politics Annual, California Journal Press, 1714 Capitol Avenue, Sacramento, CA 95814.

California Journal Almanac of State Government and Politics, published every two years by the California Center for Research and Education in Government, 1714 Capitol Avenue, Sacramento, CA 95814.

California Political Almanac, Walters, Dan, Ed., 2nd edition, Pacific Data Resources, c/o Intellimation, Inc., P.O. Box 1922, Santa Barbara, CA 93116-1922, 1990.

California Roster for (year), California state, county, city, and township officials and state officials of the United States. Directory of state services. Compiled by the secretary of state. Published every two years. Department of General Services, Office of Procurement, Publications Unit, P.O. Box 1015, North Highlands, CA 95660.

Choices for the Unincorporated Community: A Guide to Local Government Alternatives in California, 2nd edition, 1981. Institute of Governmental Affairs, Shields Library, University of California, Davis, Davis, CA 95616.

Citizen's Guide to the California Environmental Quality Act, 1985. Planning and Conservation League Foundation, 909 Twelfth Street, #203, Sacramento, CA 95814.

Constitution of the United States, Constitution of California and related documents. Legislative Bill Room, State Capitol, Sacramento, CA 95814.

Deering's California Codes, Annotated (all California codes), Bancroft-Whitney, 301 Brannan Street, San Francisco, CA 94107.

Money Can't Buy You Love, February 1991, California Common Cause, 926 J Street, CA 95814.

What's So Special About Special Districts?, Manatt, April, June 1991, Senate Local Government Committee, State Capitol, Sacramento, CA 95814.

West's Annotated California Codes (all California Codes), West Publishing Company, 50 Kellogg Boulevard, St. Paul, MN 55102.

ADDITIONAL INFORMATION FROM THE LEAGUE OF WOMEN VOTERS OF CALIFORNIA

These and other League publications may be available from your local League of Women Voters or your local library. For a current publications catalogue write to: **The League of Women Voters of California, 926 J Street #1000, Sacramento, CA 95814, or call (916) 442-7215**

PUBLICATIONS

Choosing the President 1992 — a newly revised guide to understanding the presidential election process. A League of Women Voters of California Education Fund publication. 1992.

Courts, Judges, and Voters — describes the court systems' criteria used in choosing judges and how to find the help needed to cast informed ballots. A LWVC Education Fund publication. 1990.

Voters' Guide to Judicial Elections — a brief version of the information in ***Courts, Judges, and Voters***. 1990.

California Redistricting in the 1990's — the history, process, role of the legislature, and protection of the public's interest in reapportionment. 1988.

Pros and Cons of State Ballot Measures, published approximately three months prior to each statewide election.

VIDEOTAPES

Cleaning Up Toxics at Home (25 minutes). How to use and dispose of household toxics safely, 1990.

Cleaning Up Toxics in Business (25 minutes). What small businesses are doing to prevent pollution, 1990.

It's No Surprise! Political Boundaries Are Changing (13 minutes). A Senate Elections and Reapportionment Committee videotape to inform viewers about reapportionment and redistricting, 1990.

INDEX

ORDER FORM

	Quantity	Price ea	Total
Guide to California Government		$8.95	
Shipping/Handling *See chart below			
California residents please add local sales tax			
TOTAL			

Shipping/Handling Charges:

$ .00 -	10.00	$2.90
$10.01 -	30.00	$3.25
$30.01 -	55.00	$3.45
$55.01 -	actual shipping cost	

Name _____

Address _____

City _____ State _____ Zip _____

County _____ Telephone (___) _____

Please make check payable to: League of Women Voters of California Education Fund

Mail to: LWVCEF
926 J Street, Suite 1000
Sacramento, CA 95814

For more information, please call (916) 442-7215